Sabbath Rest
Finding Peace and Reflection in God's Pre

Sabbath Rest Finding Peace and Reflection in God's Presence

Michael Stowe

Published by Heatherstone Venture Publishers, 2024.

While every precaution has been taken in the preparation of this book, the publisher assumes no responsibility for errors or omissions, or for damages resulting from the use of the information contained herein.

SABBATH REST, FINDING PEACE AND REFLECTION IN GOD'S PRESENCE

First edition. October 7, 2024.

Copyright © 2024 Michael Stowe.

Written by Michael Stowe.

Dedication

To my beautiful wife, Catherine, for your unwavering support, encouragement, and love. Your belief in me has been my greatest strength and inspiration on this journey.

To my family, whose love and support have been the foundation of my efforts. Your encouragement and understanding have been invaluable. You were in my thoughts and prayers as I wrote.

Thank you to the Cross Lutheran Community in Yorkville, Illinois, for believing in me and the vision of this book. Your faith and encouragement in my abilities have been a tremendous blessing.

Thanks to Erik, Matt, Kevin, Kristin, Russ, and Lisa for your insightful and engaging conversations. Your wisdom and reflections have profoundly encouraged my thinking and writing.

Peace and love to you all.

Michael

Sabbath Rest
Finding Peace and Reflection in God's Presence

Introduction

In the fast-paced, always-connected world we live in today, the concept of rest can feel elusive and almost impossible to grasp. The constant barrage of responsibilities, notifications, and to-do lists leaves little room for us to pause and reflect truly. We often find ourselves caught in an endless cycle of activity driven by the demands of work, family, and social obligations. This relentless pace can lead to burnout, stress, and a profound disconnection from what truly matters. Yet, amid this busyness, God has provided a timeless gift—a day of rest known as the Sabbath.

The Sabbath is more than just a day off from work; it is a sacred invitation to step away from the relentless demands of daily life and find refuge in God's presence. Observed on the seventh day, the Sabbath is a divinely ordained pause button, offering us a chance to reset, renew, and refocus our lives on what is truly important. The Sabbath is not just about physical rest, though that is certainly a crucial aspect. It is an opportunity for spiritual, emotional, and mental renewal. Setting aside one day each week to cease our labors reminds us of God's sovereignty and provision. We acknowledge that our worth and identity are not solely tied to our productivity but are rooted in our relationship with our Creator.

This divine rest offers a holistic renewal that reconnects us with God, ourselves, and our loved ones. It is a time to reflect on God's goodness, to celebrate His creation, and to experience the peace and joy that come from being in His presence. The Sabbath is a gift that allows us to recharge our spirits, strengthen our faith, and build deeper, more meaningful relationships with those around us. The Sabbath is a counter-cultural act of trust and obedience in a world that never stops. It declares that we believe in a God who cares for and provides for our needs. By honoring the Sabbath, we make a powerful statement that our lives are not defined by our busyness but by our relationship with the One who created us.

The Need for Rest

The need for rest is deeply embedded in our human nature. From the beginning of creation, God established a rhythm of work and rest. In Genesis 2:2-3, we read that God rested on the seventh day after completing His work of creation. This act of divine rest was not out of necessity but to set a precedent for us to follow. God sanctified the seventh day by resting, making it holy and distinct from the other days of the week.

Rest is essential for our well-being. It allows our bodies to recover, our minds to rejuvenate, and our spirits to reconnect with God. Without regular rest, we become overwhelmed, stressed, and disconnected from our true source of strength and peace. The Sabbath is God's provision for us to find balance, renewal, and restoration in life's busyness.

The Sabbath in Christian Practice

Throughout history, the term "Sabbath" has often been applied to Sunday to recognize the day of Christ's resurrection. The early church significantly shifted from observing the Sabbath on the seventh day (Saturday) to gathering for worship on the first day of the week (Sunday). This transition was rooted in deep theological symbolism and practical considerations.

Sunday, often referred to as the Lord's Day, became a special time for Christians to celebrate the resurrection of Jesus Christ. The shift was not merely about changing a day but about honoring the pivotal event of Christ's victory over death. Gathering on Sunday allowed early Christians to focus on the new creation and life brought forth by the resurrection. This day allowed believers to receive spiritual nourishment, strengthen their bonds as a community, and express their unity in Christ.

While the specific day is not the central focus, setting aside time for worship, reflection, and rest remains vital. As you participate in corporate worship on Sundays, remember this practice's rich history and spiritual significance.

Recognize that you are part of a long tradition of believers who have found renewal and strength in gathering to celebrate Christ's resurrection.

How to Use This Devotional

"Sabbath Rest Finding Peace and Reflection in God's Presence" devotional is designed to help you fully embrace this gift of rest. Each week, you will be guided through Scripture, reflections, practical applications, prayers, and Sabbath practices that will help you integrate the principles of Sabbath rest into your daily life. As you journey through this devotional, may you discover the profound blessings of rest and renewal that God has in store for you. May you find the peace that surpasses all understanding as you rest in His presence and draw closer to His heart.

In addition to the weekly reflections, this book includes a special section of "5th Sunday" reflections, which can be found at the end of the book. These reflections are not date-specific and can be used in any month with five Sundays. They offer deeper insights and overarching themes that complement the regular weekly reflections. The "5th Sunday" reflections provide an opportunity to explore additional aspects of Sabbath rest and to enhance your spiritual journey with fresh perspectives.

Using the 5th Sunday Reflections

To use the "5th Sunday" reflections, turn to the designated section at the end of the book whenever you encounter a month with five Sundays. These reflections are designed to fit seamlessly into your weekly routine, offering unique themes that can deepen your Sabbath experience. By incorporating these reflections, you can ensure that each Sabbath remains a time of intentional rest, reflection, and renewal, no matter the structure of the calendar month.

The "5th Sunday" reflections are a valuable addition to your Sabbath practice, allowing you to examine the overarching themes and gain deeper insights. Use these reflections to explore new aspects of your faith, find renewed inspiration, and draw closer to God. Whether focusing on the joy of worship, the power of forgiveness, or the peace of God's Word, these reflections will enrich your spiritual journey and help you make the most of your Sabbath rest.

May this book be a guide and companion as you journey through the year, finding peace and reflection in God's presence each Sabbath. Let the rhythm of rest transform your life, drawing you closer to God and enriching your spiritual walk.

Structure of the Book

"The 7th Day" is designed to guide you through a year of intentional Sabbath rest and reflection. The book consists of 52 weekly entries, each centered around a verse from the ESV Bible that pertains to rest and the Sabbath. Each entry is structured as follows:

- **Title for the Week:** A brief title that encapsulates the theme for the week.
- **Scripture Verse:** A selected verse from the ESV Bible that focuses on rest or the Sabbath.
- **Reflection:** A thoughtful meditation on the verse, connecting it to the broader theme of Sabbath rest.
- **Practical Application:** Suggestions for incorporating the principle of rest into your daily life.
- **Prayer:** A short prayer focusing on reflection and practical application.
- **Sabbath Practice:** A suggested activity or ritual during the Sabbath to foster rest and reflection.
- **Reflect and Renew:** Wrapping up the week with meaningful reflections and uplifting encouragement to guide you in the days ahead.

Monthly Themes

All entries are organized by monthly themes for a richer understanding of Sabbath rest. Each month delves into a distinct facet of rest, inviting you on a year-long exploration from diverse perspectives.

January: The Foundation of Rest

- Explore the biblical basis for rest and the Sabbath, beginning with God's example in creation.

February: Trusting in God's Timing

- Learn to trust God's perfect timing and find Peace in His plan for rest in your life.

March: Jesus and the Sabbath

- Reflect on Jesus' teachings and actions regarding the Sabbath and how they inform our understanding of rest.

April: The Sabbath as Worship

- Discover how Sabbath rest is an act of worship and devotion to God.

May: Finding Peace in Rest

- Focus on the peace that comes from resting in God's presence and promises.

June: The Rhythm of Rest

- Establish a balanced rhythm of work and rest in your daily life.

July: Rest in God's Creation

- Connect with God through the beauty and tranquility of His creation.

August: Spiritual Renewal through Rest

- Experience spiritual refreshment and renewal through prayer, meditation, and fasting.

September: Rest as Trust

- Deepen your trust in God's provision and faithfulness through intentional rest.

October: The Eternal Rest

- Contemplate the promise of eternal rest and the hope of heaven.

November: Community and Rest

- Explore the role of community and fellowship in experiencing Sabbath rest.

December: Celebrating Rest

- Celebrate the joy and blessings of rest as you reflect on God's goodness.

Inviting You to Begin the Journey

As you embark on this journey through "The 7th Day," you are invited to experience the transformative power of Sabbath rest. This devotional is not just a book to read but a guide to living a life marked by the rhythms of work and rest that God has established. Each week, you will delve into Scriptures that illuminate the importance of rest, reflect on their meaning, and apply their wisdom to your daily life.

Through these weekly reflections, prayers, and practices, you will discover the profound impact that intentional rest can have on your relationship with God, sense of peace, and overall well-being. You are about to undertake the renewal, healing, and deepened faith journey.

I encourage you to approach each entry with an open heart and a willingness to embrace the gift of rest. Allow the truths you encounter to permeate your soul and transform your life. As you set aside time each week to rest and reflect, you will find that the Sabbath is not just a day but a lifestyle that brings you closer to God's heart and aligns your life with His divine rhythm.

May this journey through "The 7th Day" be a blessing and inspiration for you. May you find the rest your soul longs for and the peace surpassing all understanding. As you begin this journey, know you are not alone; countless believers have walked this path before you, finding solace and strength in practicing Sabbath rest.

Welcome to a year of renewal, reflection, and rest. May you be richly blessed as you honor the Sabbath and draw nearer to God. Let's begin this transformative journey together, embracing the gift of rest that He graciously provides.

January: The Foundation of Rest

Week 1: The Gift of Rest - Genesis 2:2-3
Week 2: Remember the Sabbath - Exodus 20:8-11
Week 3: God's Provision in Rest - Exodus 16:23-30
Week 4: The Purpose of the Sabbath - Deuteronomy 5:12-15

February: Trusting in God's Timing

Week 5: Resting in God's Timing - Ecclesiastes 3:1-8
Week 6: The Lord's Timing is Perfect - Psalm 31:14-15
Week 7: Be Still and Know - Psalm 46:10
Week 8: God's Plan for Rest - Jeremiah 29:11

March: Jesus and the Sabbath

Week 9: Jesus, Lord of the Sabbath - Mark 2:27-28
Week 10: Healing on the Sabbath - Luke 13:10-17
Week 11: The Sabbath Made for Man - Mark 2:27
Week 12: Rest in Jesus' Teaching - Matthew 11:28-30

April: The Sabbath as Worship

Week 13: Worship and Rest - Psalm 95:1-7
Week 14: Sabbath and Sacrifice - Isaiah 1:13-17
Week 15: A Day for Worship - Leviticus 23:3
Week 16: The Joy of the Sabbath - Nehemiah 8:10-12

May: Finding Peace in Rest

Week 17: Peace in God's Presence - John 14:27
Week 18: Rest for the Soul - Psalm 62:1-2
Week 19: The Peace of Christ - Colossians 3:15
Week 20: Casting Cares on Him - 1 Peter 5:7

June: The Rhythm of Rest

Week 21: Work and Rest Balance - Exodus 34:21
Week 22: Daily Rest in God - Matthew 6:25-34
Week 23: Weekly Sabbath - Leviticus 25:4
Week 24: Annual Sabbath Rest - Leviticus 25:8-12

July: Rest in God's Creation

Week 25: The Beauty of Creation - Psalm 19:1-6
Week 26: Sabbath and Creation - Genesis 1:31-2:3
Week 27: Enjoying God's Creation - Psalm 104:24-30
Week 28: Stewardship and Rest - Genesis 2:15

August: Spiritual Renewal through Rest

Week 29: Renewal in God's Word - Psalm 119:114-117
Week 30: Spiritual Refreshment - Isaiah 40:29-31
Week 31: Renewal in Prayer - Matthew 6:6
Week 32: Rest and Fasting - Isaiah 58:6-12

September: Rest as Trust

Week 33: Trust in God's Provision - Matthew 6:31-33
Week 34: Trusting God's Plans - Proverbs 3:5-6
Week 35: Leaning on God's Strength - Isaiah 40:28-31
Week 36: Rest in God's Faithfulness - Lamentations 3:22-24

October: The Eternal Rest

Week 37: The Promise of Eternal Rest - Hebrews 4:9-10
Week 38: The Hope of Heaven - Revelation 14:13
Week 39: Rest in God's Kingdom - Matthew 25:34
Week 40: Eternal Sabbath - Revelation 21:3-4

November: Community and Rest

Week 41: Sabbath in Community - Acts 2:42-47
Week 42: Encouraging One Another - Hebrews 10:24-25
Week 43: Bearing Each Other's Burdens - Galatians 6:2
Week 44: Fellowship and Rest - 1 Thessalonians 5:11

December: Celebrating Rest

Week 45: The Joy of Rest - Zephaniah 3:17
Week 46: Celebrating God's Goodness - Psalm 92:1-4
Week 47: Rest in Thanksgiving - 1 Thessalonians 5:16-18
Week 48: Reflecting on God's Gifts - James 1:17

5th Sunday Reflections

5th Sunday reflections provide deeper insights and overarching themes that complement the regular weekly reflections. Use these reflections on months with five Sundays to enrich your spiritual journey and enhance your Sabbath observance.

January: The Foundation of Rest

Week 1: The Gift of Rest

Scripture Verse:

Genesis 2:2-3 (ESV) - "And on the seventh day God finished His work that He had done, and He rested on the seventh day from all His work that He had done. So God blessed the seventh day and made it holy because on it God rested from all His work that He had done in creation."

Reflection:

The concept of rest is rooted in the very fabric of creation. God Himself rested on the seventh day, setting a precedent for us. This divine rest was not out of necessity but to set an example for us to follow. The seventh day is sanctified, a time to cease our labors and reflect on God's goodness and the work He has accomplished. This rest reminds us of our relationship with the Creator, who made everything and provided a rhythm of work and rest for our well-being.

By resting, God showed that rest is integral to the created order. It's a time to step back, appreciate the beauty of creation, and find joy in what has been completed. When we rest, we recognize that our ultimate worth is not in what we produce but in being children of God. Resting allows us to recharge, gain perspective, and be reminded of God's sovereignty and provision.

Practical Application:

Take time this week to identify areas in your life where you can intentionally cease from your labors. Whether setting aside specific hours each day to unplug from work or dedicating a full day to rest and family, make a plan to honor the Sabbath. Consider how you can reduce distractions and create a peaceful environment that allows you to relax and recharge. Please make a list of activities that refresh your spirit and plan to incorporate them into your Sabbath routine.

- **Evaluate Your Schedule:** Look at your daily and weekly routines. Identify moments when you can step back from work and engage in restful activities.
- **Unplug from Technology:** Choose specific times to disconnect from digital devices. Use this time to focus on activities that rejuvenate your mind and spirit.
- **Create a Restful Environment:** Dedicate a space in your home where you can relax and reflect. Fill this space with things that bring you peace and joy, such as comfortable seating, soothing music, or inspiring books.

Prayer:

"Heavenly Father, thank You for the gift of rest. Help me to follow Your example and set aside time to cease from my labors and focus on You. May my rest reflect my trust in Your provision and sovereignty. Teach me to embrace the rhythm of work and rest that You have ordained. In Jesus' name, Amen."

Sabbath Practice:

Create a peaceful indoor environment where you can reflect on God's creation and rest in His presence.

- **Candle Meditation:** Light a candle and spend time in quiet reflection. Focus on the warmth and light of the candle as a symbol of God's presence. Let this time be an opportunity to thank God for the beauty of His creation and the rest He offers.
- **Reflective Reading:** Choose a book or passage from the Bible that speaks to God's creation and rest. Spend time reading and meditating on the words, allowing them to draw you closer to God's peace.

Reflect and Renew:

As you begin this journey of embracing the Sabbath, remember that rest is a divine gift meant to restore and refresh you. Each week, take intentional steps to incorporate rest into your life, trusting that God's rhythm of work and rest is designed for your well-being. May this week be the start of a transformative journey toward deeper peace and connection with God.

Week 2: Remember the Sabbath

Scripture Verse:

Exodus 20:8-11 (ESV) - "Remember the Sabbath day, to keep it holy. Six days you shall labor and do all your work, but the seventh day is a Sabbath to the LORD your God. On it, you shall not do any work, you, or your son, or your daughter, your male servant, or your female servant, or your livestock, or the sojourner who is within your gates. For in six days the LORD made heaven and earth, the sea, and all that is in them, and rested on the seventh day. Therefore the LORD blessed the Sabbath day and made it holy."

Reflection:

The command to remember and keep the Sabbath holy is vital to God's law. This commandment invites us to set aside our regular work and dedicate one day each week to rest and spiritual renewal. The Sabbath is a sign of the covenant between God and His people, reminding us that we belong to Him. Observing the Sabbath, we acknowledge God's authority over our time and trust in His provision. It is a day to focus on our relationship with God, family, and community.

Observing the Sabbath helps us maintain a healthy balance between work and rest. It allows us to pause, reflect on our lives, and reconnect with God. This holy rest is not only about physical cessation from labor but also about spiritual refreshment. It is a time to delight in God's creation, express gratitude for His blessings, and deepen our faith.

Practical Application:

Take time this week to plan how you will observe the Sabbath. Consider how you can honor this day and make it special.

- **Evaluate Your Schedule:** Look at your daily and weekly routines. Identify moments when you can step back from work and engage in restful activities.
- **Unplug from Technology:** Choose specific times to disconnect from digital devices. Use this time to focus on activities that rejuvenate your mind and spirit.
- **Create a Restful Environment:** Dedicate a space in your home where you can relax and reflect. Fill this space with things that bring you peace and joy, such as comfortable seating, soothing music, or inspiring books.

Prayer:

"Lord, thank You for the gift of the Sabbath. Help me to remember and keep it holy. Teach me to rest in You and to trust in Your provision. May this day be a time of renewal and deepening my relationship with You. In Jesus' name, Amen."

Sabbath Practice:

Engage in practices that help you experience the blessing of the Sabbath without leaving your home.

- **Create a Cozy Sabbath Corner:** Dedicate a space in your home for Sabbath rest. Add soft blankets, pillows, and calming scents like lavender. Use this space to pray, read, or simply sit in God's presence.
- **Sabbath Journaling:** Reflect on your experiences of rest and renewal. Write down your thoughts, prayers, and any insights you gain as you intentionally observe the Sabbath

Reflect and Renew:

As you begin to observe the Sabbath more intentionally, remember that this day is a gift from God meant to bring rest and renewal. Each week, take steps to keep the Sabbath holy, trusting that God's rhythm of work and rest is designed for your well-being. May this week deepen your peace and connection with God.

Week 3: God's Provision in Rest

Scripture Verse:

Psalm 23:1-3 (ESV) - "The Lord is my shepherd; I shall not want. He makes me lie down in green pastures. He leads me beside still waters. He restores my soul. He leads me in paths of righteousness for his name's sake."

Reflection:

Psalm 23 is a beautiful reminder of God's provision and care for us. As our shepherd, He guides us to places of rest and refreshment. The imagery of lying down in green pastures and being led beside still waters evokes a sense of peace and tranquility. This rest is not only physical but also spiritual, as God restores our souls and leads us in righteousness.

Trusting in God's provision means recognizing that He knows our needs and provides for them. When we rest, we acknowledge that our security and well-being come from God, not from our own efforts. This allows us to release our anxieties and find peace in His care.

Practical Application:

Focus on trusting God's provision in your life this week. Consider how you can rest in His care and release your anxieties.

- **Plan Your Meals:** Plan and prepare your meals ahead of time so that you can rest on the Sabbath without worrying about cooking.
- **Trust in God's Provision:** Reflect on areas in your life where you need to trust God's provision. Write down these areas and pray over them, asking God to help you rely on His sufficiency.
- **Simplify Your Schedule:** Look for ways to lighten your workload leading up to the Sabbath. This might mean delegating tasks, prioritizing what needs to be done, and letting go of less important activities.

Prayer:

"Lord, thank You for being my shepherd and providing for all my needs. Help me to trust in Your care and to find rest in Your provision. Restore my soul and lead me in paths of righteousness. In Jesus' name, Amen."

Sabbath Practice:

Focus on remembering God's provision through indoor activities.

- **Gratitude List:** Create a list of things you are grateful for, focusing on how God has provided for you. Reflect on this list during your Sabbath time, thanking God for His blessings.
- **Indoor Worship:** Spend time listening to worship music that reminds you of God's provision. Sing along or simply sit and soak in the lyrics, allowing them to deepen your trust in God's care.

Reflect and Renew:

As you rest in God's provision, remember that He cares for you and knows your needs. Each week, trust in His sufficiency and find peace in His care. May this week deepen your reliance on God and your sense of peace in His presence.

Week 4: The Purpose of the Sabbath

Scripture Verse:

Deuteronomy 5:12-15 (ESV) - "Observe the Sabbath day, to keep it holy, as the Lord your God commanded you. Six days you shall labor and do all your work, but the seventh day is a Sabbath to the Lord your God. On it you shall not do any work, you or your son or your daughter or your male servant or your female servant or your ox or your donkey or any of your livestock or the sojourner who is within your gates, that your male servant and your female servant may rest as well as you. You shall remember that you were a slave in the land of Egypt, and the Lord your God brought you out from there with a mighty hand and an outstretched arm. Therefore the Lord your God commanded you to keep the Sabbath day."

Reflection:

The command to observe the Sabbath day and keep it holy is rooted in God's deliverance of His people from slavery in Egypt. The Sabbath is a reminder of God's mighty hand and outstretched arm that brought freedom and rest. It is a day to cease from labor and remember God's saving acts, to rest in His grace and reflect on His faithfulness.

The Sabbath is not only about physical rest but also about spiritual liberation. It is a time to remember that we are no longer slaves to our work, our schedules, or our anxieties. We are free in Christ to rest and rejoice in His provision and salvation.

Practical Application:

This week, focus on the purpose of the Sabbath as a time to remember and celebrate God's deliverance.

- **Reflect on God's Faithfulness:** Spend time reflecting on how God has delivered you from difficult situations in your life. Write down these instances and thank God for His faithfulness.
- **Family Stories:** Share stories of God's faithfulness with your family. Use the Sabbath as an opportunity to build a family tradition of remembering and celebrating God's goodness.
- **Acts of Gratitude:** Perform acts of gratitude, such as writing thank-you notes to people who have been blessings in your life or engaging in a service project to honor God's deliverance and provision.

Prayer:

"Lord, thank You for the Sabbath and for delivering me from the bondage of sin and anxiety. Help me to remember Your faithfulness and to rest in Your grace. May this day be a time of celebration and reflection on Your mighty works. In Jesus' name, Amen."

Sabbath Practice:

Rest in God's sovereignty by engaging in peaceful, reflective activities indoors.

- **Breathing Meditation:** Practice deep breathing exercises while meditating on God's sovereignty. As you inhale, focus on God's control over every aspect of your life. As you exhale, release any worries or anxieties, trusting them into God's hands.
- **Scripture Art:** Create a piece of art that reflects your favorite verse about God's sovereignty. This could be as simple as writing the verse in calligraphy or drawing a small illustration. Let this creative time be an act of worship and reflection.

Reflect and Renew:

As you observe the Sabbath, remember that it is a gift from God meant to remind you of His deliverance and faithfulness. Each week, take time to reflect on His mighty works and to rest in His grace. May this week deepen your gratitude and joy in God's provision.

Summary of January: The Foundation of Rest

The theme for January is "The Foundation of Rest." Throughout this month, we have focused on understanding the biblical basis for rest, the importance of the Sabbath, and how God's provision and faithfulness are integral to our rest.

Reflecting on the Month:

As you reflect on the past month, consider how establishing a foundation of rest has impacted your life. How has focusing on God's provision, faithfulness, and the purpose of the Sabbath brought renewal and restoration to your spirit? Have you experienced a deeper sense of peace and connection with God?

- **Personal Reflections:** Spend time journaling about your experiences this month. What have you learned about the foundation of rest? How have these insights changed your approach to rest and work?
- **Gratitude:** Reflect on the ways God's foundation of rest has blessed you. Write down the moments when you felt the most refreshed and thank Him for His guidance.

Invitation to Continue the Journey:

The journey of establishing a foundation of rest is ongoing. As you move forward, carry with you the lessons and practices you have developed this month. Continue to seek a balanced rhythm in your daily life, trusting in God's provision and finding renewal through the Sabbath.

- **Ongoing Practice:** Make rest a regular part of your routine. Keep focusing on balancing work and rest, practicing daily trust, and observing the Sabbath with intentionality.
- **Community Sharing:** Share your insights and experiences with your faith community. Encourage others to embrace the foundation of rest and to find renewal in God's design for rest and work.

May the foundation you have built this month continue to support and enrich your journey throughout the year. Embrace each day and each Sabbath with a renewed sense of balance, peace, and connection with God. Let His foundation of rest guide you into deeper renewal and fulfillment.

Looking Ahead:

As you prepare to move into the next month of "Sabbath Rest: Finding Peace and Reflection in God's Presence," look forward to exploring new themes and insights about the Sabbath. Each month builds upon the previous one, offering a richer and more profound understanding of rest and renewal.

In February, we will focus on "Trusting in God's Timing," exploring how God's perfect timing brings rest and peace to our lives. May you be blessed as you continue this journey, finding ever deeper peace and joy in the gift of the Sabbath.

February: Trusting in God's Timing

Week 5: Resting in God's Timing

Scripture Verse:

Ecclesiastes 3:1-8 (ESV) - "For everything, there is a season, and a time for every matter under heaven: a time to be born, and a time to die; a time to plant, and a time to pluck up what is planted; a time to kill, and a time to heal; a time to break down, and a time to build up; a time to weep, and a time to laugh; a time to mourn, and a time to dance; a time to cast away stones, and a time to gather stones together; a time to embrace, and a time to refrain from embracing; a time to seek, and a time to lose; a time to keep, and a time to cast away; a time to tear, and a time to sew; a time to keep silence, and a time to speak; a time to love, and a time to hate; a time for war, and a time for peace."

Reflection:

This beautiful passage from Ecclesiastes reminds us that life is composed of various seasons, each with its own time and purpose. In His wisdom, God has appointed a time for every matter under heaven. Understanding and accepting this divine timing is crucial to finding peace and rest. Our struggles and frustrations often arise from trying to force events according to our timelines rather than trusting God's perfect timing.

Resting in God's timing means surrendering our schedules, plans, and desires to Him. It requires faith to believe that God knows what is best for us and that His timing is always perfect. When we align ourselves with God's timing, we experience a profound sense of peace and assurance, knowing that every season has its place and purpose in His grand design.

Practical Application:

This week, focus on trusting God's timing in different areas of your life. Reflect on surrendering your timelines and plans to His perfect will.

- **Identify Areas of Control:** Take some time to identify areas in your life where you are trying to control the timing of events. Write these down and pray for the strength to surrender them to God.
- **Reflect on Past Seasons:** Reflect on past seasons of your life and how God's timing was evident. Write about these experiences and how they have shaped your faith and trust in Him.
- **Daily Surrender:** Start each day with a prayer of surrender, asking God to help you trust His timing for the events and tasks you will face.

Prayer:

"Lord, thank You for the wisdom and assurance that You have appointed a time for every matter under heaven. Help me to trust Your timing and surrender my plans to You. Teach me to rest in the knowledge that You are in control, and give me the patience to wait for Your perfect timing. May Your Peace fill my heart as I align my life with Your divine seasons. In Jesus' name, Amen."

Sabbath Practice:

Spend time this Sabbath reflecting on the different seasons of your life and how God has been present in each one.

- **Seasonal Reflection:** Take a walk in nature or find a quiet place to sit and reflect. Consider the natural seasons—winter, spring, summer, and fall—and how they mirror your life's seasons. Reflect on the growth, change, and rest that each season brings.
- **Create a Timeline:** Draw a timeline of your life, marking significant events and seasons. Reflect on how God's timing was evident in each phase. Use this time to thank God for His guidance and provision through all seasons.

Reflect and Renew:

Trusting in God's timing brings a deep sense of peace and rest. As you reflect on the seasons of your life, remember that God has appointed a time for everything. Embrace each season with faith, knowing that God's timing is perfect and His plans for you are good. Let this Sabbath be a time of surrender and trust as you rest in the assurance of His divine timing.

Week 6: The Lord's Timing is Perfect

Scripture Verse:

Psalm 31:14-15 (ESV) - "But I trust in you, O LORD; I say, 'You are my God.' My times are in your hand; rescue me from the hand of my enemies and from my persecutors!"

Reflection:

Psalm 31 is a powerful reminder of God's sovereignty over our lives. David trusts the Lord, acknowledging that his times are in God's hands. This declaration is about general trust and trusting God's timing in trials and adversities. David's confidence in God's perfect timing gives him the strength to endure difficulties and wait patiently for God's deliverance.

Trusting in God's timing means believing He knows what is best for us, even when circumstances seem overwhelming. It requires us to let go of our need to control every aspect of our lives and to place our times—our past, present, and future—into God's capable hands. This trust brings peace, knowing that God's timing is perfect and His plans for us are good.

Practical Application:

This week, focus on areas where you struggle to trust God's timing. Practice surrendering these areas to Him and look for ways to build trust in His perfect plan.

- **Identify Struggles:** Identify specific situations where you find it hard to trust God's timing. Write these down and reflect on why it is difficult to surrender these areas.
- **Scripture Meditation:** Spend time each day meditating on Psalm 31:14-15. Let the words sink into your heart and remind you of God's sovereignty and care.
- **Affirmation of Trust:** Create a personal affirmation based on Psalm 31:14-15, such as "My times are in Your hands, Lord." Repeat this affirmation throughout the day whenever you feel anxious or impatient.

Prayer:

"Lord, I trust in You and declare You are my God. My times are in Your hands. Help me to release my anxieties and impatience into Your care, knowing that Your timing is perfect. Rescue me from my fears and help me to rest in Your sovereign plan. Strengthen my faith and trust in You. In Jesus' name, Amen."

Sabbath Practice:

Engage in a Sabbath activity focusing on reflecting and trusting God's perfect timing.

- **Trust Walk:** Take a leisurely walk in a place that brings you peace, such as a park or along a quiet path. As you

walk, think about areas where you need to trust God's timing. Use this time to pray and release your concerns to Him.
- **Timeline Journal:** Reflect on key moments where you have seen God's perfect timing at work. Write these moments in a journal, detailing how God's timing was evident and how it brought about His good purposes.

Reflect and Renew:
Trusting in the Lord's timing brings peace and assurance, even during challenges. As you reflect on Psalm 31 and your life experiences, remember that your times are in God's hands. He knows your needs, desires, and the perfect timing for everything. Embrace this trust and let it guide you to a place of rest and peace, knowing that God's timing is always perfect.

Week 7: Be Still and Know

Scripture Verse:
Psalm 46:10 (ESV) - "Be still, and know that I am God. I will be exalted among the nations, I will be exalted in the earth!"

Reflection:
Psalm 46:10 is a powerful invitation to stop striving and recognize God's sovereignty. In a world where busyness and productivity are often equated with worth, this verse calls us to pause and find our value in God's presence. "Be still" is not just a call to physical stillness but to mental and spiritual stillness, to a calm and quiet confidence in God's control over all things.

Being still allows us to focus on God's nature and character, to remember that He is exalted above all and that His purposes will prevail. It shifts our perspective from our efforts and anxieties to God's infinite power and love. This stillness is an act of worship and trust, acknowledging that God is in control and that we can rest in His presence.

Practical Application:
This week, practice stillness in your daily routine. Find moments to pause and reflect on God's greatness and His control over your life.

- **Daily Quiet Time:** Set aside a specific time for quiet reflection and prayer each day. Use this time to be still before God, focusing on His attributes and sovereignty.
- **Mindful Breathing:** Practice mindful breathing exercises to help calm your mind and focus on God. Inhale deeply, thinking of God's Peace, and exhale slowly, releasing your worries.
- **Nature Reflection:** Spend time in a natural setting, observing the stillness and beauty of creation. Let the tranquility of nature remind you of God's presence and power.

Prayer:
"Lord, help me to be still and know that You are God. In life's busyness and challenges, teach me to pause and recognize Your sovereignty. Calm my anxious heart and fill me with Your Peace. May I find rest in Your presence and trust in Your perfect plan. In Jesus' name, Amen."

Sabbath Practice:
Incorporate a practice of stillness into your Sabbath observance, using this time to deepen your awareness of God's presence.

- **Stillness Meditation:** Dedicate a portion of your Sabbath to stillness meditation. Sit in a quiet place, close your eyes, and focus on the phrase, "Be still and know that I am God." Repeat it slowly, allowing each word to sink in and bring peace to your soul.

- **Reflective Journaling:** After meditation, journal your thoughts and reflections. Write about how being still before God has impacted your perspective and brought you closer to Him.

Reflect and Renew:

Being still before God is a profound act of trust and worship. It allows us to step back from our efforts and anxieties and to recognize God's supreme authority and love. As you practice stillness this week, may you experience the peace and assurance that comes from knowing that God is in control. Let this stillness draw you nearer to Him and deepen your trust in His perfect plan.

Week 8: God's Plan for Rest

Scripture Verse:

Jeremiah 29:11 (ESV) - "For I know the plans I have for you, declares the LORD, plans for welfare and not for evil, to give you a future and a hope."

Reflection:

Jeremiah 29:11 is a beloved verse that assures us of God's good plans for our lives. Although originally spoken to the Israelites in exile, its message of hope and trust in God's providence is timeless. This verse reminds us that God's plans are always for our welfare, to give us a future and hope, even when our current circumstances are challenging.

Resting in God's plan involves trusting His intentions for us, which are good, even when we do not understand our present situation. It requires faith to believe God is at work behind the scenes, orchestrating events for our benefit. This kind of trust brings peace and allows us to rest, knowing that we are in the hands of a loving and sovereign God.

Practical Application:

This week, focus on trusting and resting in God's plans for your life, even when circumstances are uncertain or difficult.

- **Identify Your Worries:** Write down the areas of your life where you feel anxious or uncertain about the future. In prayer, bring these concerns to God, asking Him to help you trust His plans.
- **Scripture Memorization:** Memorize Jeremiah 29:11 and repeat it yourself whenever you feel anxious about the future. Let the truth of God's good plans bring you comfort and peace.
- **Plan with Faith:** When making plans for the future, do so with trust in God's sovereignty. Acknowledge that while you can make plans, God directs your steps.

Prayer:

"Heavenly Father, thank You for Your promise of good plans for my life. Help me trust in Your providence and rest in the assurance that You are working all things for my good. Give me peace as I surrender my worries and uncertainties to You, knowing that my future is secure in Your hands. In Jesus' name, Amen."

Sabbath Practice:

Dedicate this Sabbath to reflecting on God's plans for your life and finding Peace in His sovereignty.

- **Future Visioning:** Imagine your future while meditating on God's promise in Jeremiah 29:11. Write down your hopes and dreams, then pray over them, asking God to align your plans with His.
- **Thanksgiving Reflection:** Reflect on past instances where God's plans were evident in your life. Write a list of these moments and thank God for His faithfulness and guidance.

Reflect and Renew:

Trusting in God's plan brings profound peace and rest. Jeremiah 29:11 reminds us that God's intentions for us are always for our good, even when we cannot see the full picture. As you rest in this promise, let it transform your perspective on the future. Embrace this Sabbath confidently in God's perfect plan for your life, allowing His Peace to fill your heart and mind.

Summary of February: Trusting in God's Timing

The theme for February is "Trusting in God's Timing." This month, we have focused on understanding and embracing God's perfect timing. Each week, we explored different aspects of trusting God's timing, learning to wait patiently, and finding peace in His plans.

Reflecting on the Month

As you reflect on the past month, consider how trusting God's timing has impacted your life. How has focusing on God's sovereignty, learning to wait patiently, and trusting in His plans brought peace and assurance to your spirit? Have you experienced a deeper sense of trust and reliance on God?

- **Personal Reflections:** Spend time journaling about your experiences this month. What have you learned about trusting in God's timing? How have these insights changed your approach to waiting and trusting God's plans?
- **Gratitude:** Reflect on how trusting in God's timing has blessed you. Write down the moments when you felt the most assured, and thank God for His faithfulness and guidance.

Invitation to Continue the Journey

The journey of trusting in God's timing is ongoing. As you progress, carry the lessons and practices you have developed this month. Continue to seek God's guidance daily, trusting His perfect timing and finding peace through His plans.

- **Ongoing Practice:** Make trusting God's timing a routine. Focus on relying on His plans, practicing patience, and intentionally observing the Sabbath.
- **Community Sharing:** Share your insights and experiences with your faith community. Encourage others to trust God's timing and find peace in His plans.

May the foundation you have built this month continue to support and enrich your journey throughout the year. Embrace each day and each Sabbath with a renewed sense of trust, peace, and connection with God. Let His timing guide you into deeper assurance and fulfillment.

Looking Ahead

As you prepare to move into the next month of "The 7th Day" devotional, look forward to exploring new themes and insights about the Sabbath. Each month builds upon the previous one, offering a more profound understanding of rest and renewal.

In March, we will focus on "Jesus and the Sabbath," exploring how Jesus observed and taught about the Sabbath and what we can learn from His example. May you be blessed as you continue this journey, finding ever deeper peace and joy in the gift of the Sabbath.

March: Jesus and the Sabbath

Week 9: Jesus, Lord of the Sabbath

Scripture Verse:

Mark 2:27-28 (ESV) - "And he said to them, 'The Sabbath was made for man, not man for the Sabbath. So the Son of Man is lord even of the Sabbath.'"

Reflection:

In Mark 2:27-28, Jesus challenges the legalistic interpretations of the Sabbath held by the Pharisees. He reminds them and us that the Sabbath is a gift from God for humanity's benefit. It is not a burden but a provision for rest and renewal. Jesus asserts His authority over the Sabbath, highlighting that it is designed to serve us, not to enslave us.

Jesus, as Lord of the Sabbath, redefines its purpose. He emphasizes that the Sabbath should be a time of restoration, healing, and worship. By saying the Sabbath was made for man, Jesus affirms that God's intention was always to provide a day for physical rest and spiritual enrichment. This understanding frees us from rigid and legalistic observance and invites us into a joyful and life-giving practice of the Sabbath.

Practical Application:

This week, focus on experiencing the Sabbath as a gift rather than a burden. Reflect on how you can make the Sabbath a day of restoration and joy.

- **Evaluate Your Sabbath Observance:** Consider how you currently observe the Sabbath. Are there ways you can make it more restful and enjoyable? Reflect on your legalistic tendencies and seek to embrace the freedom Jesus offers.
- **Plan Restorative Activities:** Plan activities for the Sabbath that bring joy and restoration. This could include spending time with loved ones, engaging in a hobby, or resting.
- **Focus on Worship:** Use part of the Sabbath for intentional worship. Attend a church service, listen to worship music, pray, and read Scripture.

Prayer:

"Lord Jesus, thank You for being the Lord of the Sabbath and teaching us that the Sabbath is a gift meant for our benefit. Please help me to embrace the Sabbath with joy and gratitude, seeing it as a time for rest and restoration. Free me from legalistic tendencies and help me experience the Sabbath's true purpose. In Your name, Amen."

Sabbath Practice:

Create a Sabbath experience that focuses on restoration, joy, and worship.

- **Restorative Rest:** Dedicate a significant portion of the Sabbath to activities that restore your body and soul. This might include napping, reading a good book, or enjoying nature.
- **Joyful Worship:** Engage in worship that fills you with joy. Sing your favorite worship songs, attend a vibrant church service, or spend time in personal worship and reflection.

Reflect and Renew:

Jesus, as Lord of the Sabbath, invites us to experience it as a gift of rest and renewal. By understanding that it was made for our benefit, we can embrace it with joy and gratitude. Let this week be a time to deepen your understanding of the Sabbath and to celebrate the freedom and restoration it brings. Embrace the Sabbath as a day to rest, restore, and worship, knowing that it is a precious gift from God.

Week 10: Healing on the Sabbath

Scripture Verse:

Luke 13:10-17 (ESV) - "Now he was teaching in one of the synagogues on the Sabbath, and behold, there was a woman who had had a disabling spirit for eighteen years. She was bent over and could not fully straighten herself. When Jesus saw her, he called her over and said, 'Woman, you are freed from your disability.' And he laid his hands on her, and immediately she was made straight, and she glorified God. But the ruler of the synagogue, indignant because Jesus had healed on the Sabbath, said to the people, 'There are six days in which work ought to be done. Come on those days and be healed, not on the Sabbath day.' Then the Lord answered him, 'You hypocrites! Does not each of you on the Sabbath untie his ox or donkey from the manger and lead it away to water it? And ought not this woman, a daughter of Abraham whom Satan bound for eighteen years, be loosed from this bond on the Sabbath day?' As he said these things, all his adversaries were put to shame, and all the people rejoiced at all the glorious things that he did."

Reflection:

In this passage, Jesus heals a woman on the Sabbath, demonstrating that the Sabbath is a time for restoration and compassion. The religious leaders were more concerned with strict adherence to the Sabbath laws than with the woman's well-being. Jesus challenges this mindset, showing that the Sabbath is an appropriate time for acts of mercy and healing.

Jesus' healing on the Sabbath reveals God's heart, which is always inclined toward restoring and renewing His people. The Sabbath is about refraining from work and embracing the fullness of life that God desires for us. Acts of kindness, mercy, and healing align perfectly with the spirit of the Sabbath.

Practical Application:

This week, focus on using the Sabbath for healing and compassion for yourself and others.

- **Self-Care:** Use the Sabbath to care for your physical, emotional, and spiritual health. Engage in activities that promote healing and well-being.
- **Acts of Kindness:** Look for opportunities to show compassion to others. This could be through visiting someone lonely, helping a neighbor, or simply offering a listening ear.
- **Reflect on Healing:** Reflect on areas where you need healing. Pray and ask God to restore and renew these areas.

Prayer:

"Lord Jesus, thank You for demonstrating that the Sabbath is a time for healing and compassion. Please help me to embrace this truth and to use the Sabbath as a time to care for myself and others. Open my eyes to opportunities to show kindness and bring healing to those around me. In Your name, Amen."

Sabbath Practice:

Engage in activities that promote healing and compassion on the Sabbath.

- **Healing Walk:** Take a leisurely walk, focusing on nature's healing and restorative power. Use this time to pray for healing in your life and the lives of others.
- **Compassionate Outreach:** Plan a simple act of kindness for someone in need. This could be preparing a meal for a sick friend, visiting someone in the hospital, or writing a note of encouragement.

Reflect and Renew:

The Sabbath is a time for healing and compassion. As you observe it this week, look for ways to restore and be kind to yourself and others. Embrace the spirit of the Sabbath by engaging in acts of mercy and love, following Jesus' example.

Week 11: The Sabbath Made for Man

Scripture Verse:

Mark 2:27 (ESV) - "And he said to them, 'The Sabbath was made for man, not man for the Sabbath.'"

Reflection:

In Mark 2:27, Jesus clarifies the purpose of the Sabbath, emphasizing that it was created for humanity's benefit. The Sabbath is not meant to be a burden or a set of rigid rules but a gift that provides rest, renewal, and connection with God. This perspective shifts our understanding of the Sabbath from a legalistic requirement to a loving provision from God.

The Sabbath is an opportunity to step back from life's demands and focus on what truly matters. It is a time to rest in God's presence, rejuvenate our bodies and spirits, and reconnect with our loved ones. By observing the Sabbath, we acknowledge our need for rest and dependence on God's provision.

Practical Application:

This week, focus on experiencing the Sabbath as a gift and a time for renewal.

- **Evaluate Your Sabbath:** Reflect on how you currently observe the Sabbath. Are there ways to make it more restorative and enjoyable? Consider eliminating burdensome activities and adding those that bring joy and peace.
- **Plan Joyful Activities:** On the Sabbath, plan activities that bring joy and rest. These could include spending time with family, enjoying a hobby, or simply relaxing.
- **Focus on Gratitude:** Use the Sabbath to reflect on and express gratitude for the blessings in your life. Write down things you are thankful for and thank God for His provision.

Prayer:

"Lord, thank You for creating the Sabbath as a gift for me. Help me embrace this time of rest and renewal and see it as a joyful opportunity to connect with You and those I love. Guide me in making the Sabbath a day of true rest and rejuvenation. In Jesus' name, Amen."

Sabbath Practice:

Create a Sabbath experience that focuses on joy and gratitude.

- **Joyful Celebration:** Plan an activity that brings you and your loved ones together. This could be a special meal, a game night, or a nature outing.
- **Gratitude Journal:** Start a gratitude journal specifically for the Sabbath. Write down things you are thankful for each week and reflect on God's goodness.

Reflect and Renew:

The Sabbath was made for you as a gift from God. Embrace this time as an opportunity for rest, joy, and renewal. Let the Sabbath be a reminder of God's love and provision, and use it to reconnect with Him and those who matter most in your life.

Week 12: Rest in Jesus' Teaching

Scripture Verse:

Matthew 11:28-30 (ESV) - "Come to me, all who labor and are heavily laden, and I will give you rest. Take my yoke upon you, and learn from me, for I am gentle and lowly in heart, and you will find rest for your souls. For my yoke is easy, and my burden is light."

Reflection:

In Matthew 11:28-30, Jesus extends a personal invitation to those weary and burdened to find rest in Him. He promises that by taking His yoke and learning from Him, we will discover a gentle and restful way of living. This invitation is about physical rest and finding true rest for our souls.

Jesus offers different rest from trusting Him and walking in His ways. His yoke is easy, and His burden is light because He carries it with us. This rest is found in a relationship with Jesus, where we learn to live according to His teachings and rely on His strength. It invites us to exchange our heavy burdens for His light and gentle leadership.

Practical Application:

This week, focus on accepting Jesus' invitation to rest and learning from His gentle and humble heart.

- **Reflect on Your Burdens:** Identify your burdens and stresses. Write them down and bring them to Jesus in prayer, asking Him to help you find rest in Him.
- **Learn from Jesus:** Read the Gospels, spending time on Jesus' life and teachings. Reflect on how His way of living can bring rest to your soul.
- **Simplify Your Life:** Look for ways to simplify your schedule and responsibilities. Focus on what truly matters and let go of unnecessary burdens.

Prayer:

"Lord Jesus, thank You for inviting me to come to You and find rest. Help me to lay down my burdens and to learn from Your gentle and humble heart. Teach me to walk in Your ways and to trust in Your strength. May I find true rest for my soul in You. In Your name, Amen."

Sabbath Practice:

Embrace Jesus' invitation to rest by focusing on peace and renewal activities.

- **Quiet Time with Jesus:** Dedicate a portion of your Sabbath to spend in quiet reflection and prayer, focusing on Jesus' invitation to rest. Read Matthew 11:28-30 and meditate on its meaning for your life.
- **Simplify and Rest:** Choose a simple, restful activity that allows you to experience Jesus' Peace. This could be taking a quiet walk, reading a favorite book, or enjoying a peaceful hobby.

Reflect and Renew:

Jesus offers you rest for your soul, an invitation to exchange your burdens for His light yoke. As you observe the Sabbath this week, accept His invitation and find Peace in His gentle and humble heart. Let this time of rest draw you closer to Him and renew your spirit.

Summary of March: Jesus and the Sabbath

March's theme is "Jesus and the Sabbath." This month, we have focused on understanding how Jesus observed and taught about the Sabbath. Each week, we explored different aspects of Jesus' teachings, His example, and how His approach to the Sabbath can inspire and guide us.

Reflecting on the Month

As you reflect on the past month, consider how focusing on Jesus and the Sabbath has impacted your life. How has studying Jesus' teachings and example brought new insights into your Sabbath observance and your relationship with God? Have you experienced a deeper connection with Jesus and a greater appreciation for the Sabbath?

- **Personal Reflections:** Spend time journaling about your experiences this month. What have you learned about Jesus and the Sabbath? How have these insights changed your approach to Sabbath observance and your relationship with Jesus?
- **Gratitude:** Reflect on how Jesus' Sabbath teachings have blessed you. Write down the moments when you felt the most inspired and thank Jesus for His example and guidance.

Invitation to Continue the Journey

The journey of understanding Jesus and the Sabbath is ongoing. As you move forward, carry the lessons and practices you have developed this month. Continue to seek Jesus' guidance daily, learning from His example and finding renewal through the Sabbath.

- **Ongoing Practice:** Make learning from Jesus a regular routine. Keep focusing on His teachings, following His example, and intentionally observing the Sabbath.
- **Community Sharing:** Share your insights and experiences with your faith community. Encourage others to learn from Jesus' example and to find inspiration in His approach to the Sabbath.

May the foundation you have built this month continue to support and enrich your journey throughout the year. Embrace each day and each Sabbath with a renewed sense of inspiration, peace, and connection with Jesus. Let His teachings guide you into deeper renewal and fulfillment.

Looking Ahead

As you prepare to move into the next month of "The 7th Day" devotional, look forward to exploring new themes and insights about the Sabbath. Each month builds upon the previous one, offering a more profound understanding of rest and renewal.

In April, we will focus on "Spiritual Renewal," exploring how the Sabbath can be a time for deep spiritual growth and rejuvenation. May you be blessed as you continue this journey, finding ever deeper peace and joy in the gift of the Sabbath.

April: The Sabbath as Worship

Week 13: Worship and Rest

Scripture Verse:

Psalm 95:1-7 (ESV) - "Oh come, let us sing to the LORD; let us make a joyful noise to the rock of our salvation! Let us come into his presence with thanksgiving; let us make a joyful noise to him with songs of praise! For the LORD is a great God, and a great King above all gods. In his hand are the depths of the earth; the heights of the mountains are his also. The sea is his, for he made it, and his hands formed the dry land. Oh, come, let us worship and bow down; let us kneel before the LORD, our Maker! For he is our God, and we are the people of his pasture, and the sheep of his hand. Today, if you hear his voice, do not harden your hearts, as at Meribah, as on the day at Massah in the wilderness."

Reflection:

Psalm 95 is a beautiful call to worship and bow before the Lord. It reminds us that worship is an integral part of the Sabbath. When we set aside time to worship God, we acknowledge His greatness and our dependence on Him. Worship on the Sabbath allows us to reorient our hearts and minds toward God, celebrating His creation, provision, and salvation.

This passage encourages us to approach God with thanksgiving and praise. The Sabbath is a perfect opportunity to reflect on God's goodness and to express our gratitude for all He has done. Worship is a duty and a joyful response to God's love and faithfulness.

Practical Application:

This week, focus on making worship a central part of your Sabbath observance.

- **Morning Worship:** Start your Sabbath with a time of worship. Sing praises, read Psalm 95, and pray, thanking God for His blessings.
- **Family Worship:** If possible, gather your family for a time of worship. Sing together, read Scripture, and share what you are thankful for.
- **Worship Playlist:** Create a playlist of worship songs that uplift your spirit and draw you closer to God. Listen to it throughout the day.

Prayer:

"Lord, thank You for the gift of worship and inviting us into Your presence. Help me to make worship a central part of my Sabbath, to come before You with thanksgiving and praise. May my heart be filled with joy as I reflect on Your goodness and faithfulness. In Jesus' name, Amen."

Sabbath Practice:

Engage in a dedicated time of worship on the Sabbath.

- **Worship Walk:** Walk in nature, praising God for His creation. Sing or listen to worship music as you walk, and reflect on God's greatness.
- **Worship Reflection:** Journal about your experiences of God's goodness. Write down your praises and

thanksgiving as an act of worship.

Reflect and Renew:

Worship is an essential part of the Sabbath, helping us to connect with God and express our gratitude for His blessings. Let this week be a time of joyful worship as you come into God's presence with thanksgiving and praise.

Week 14: Sabbath and Sacrifice

Scripture Verse:

Isaiah 1:13-17 (ESV) - "Bring no more vain offerings; incense is an abomination to me. New moon and Sabbath and the calling of convocations—I cannot endure iniquity and solemn assembly. Your new moons and your appointed feasts my soul hates; they have become a burden to me; I am weary of bearing them. When you spread out your hands, I will hide my eyes from you; even though you make many prayers, I will not listen; your hands are full of blood. Wash yourselves; make yourselves clean; remove the evil of your deeds from before my eyes; cease to do evil, learn to do good; seek justice, correct oppression; bring justice to the fatherless, plead the widow's cause."

Reflection:

In this passage, God expresses His displeasure with empty religious rituals that lack true repentance and justice. The people observed the Sabbath and other spiritual practices, but their hearts were far from God. True Sabbath worship involves more than just outward observance; it requires a heart that seeks to honor God through righteous living.

Isaiah calls the people to genuine repentance and to align their actions with God's will. This means seeking justice, correcting oppression, and caring for the vulnerable. True worship on the Sabbath includes reflecting on our lives and making changes that align with God's values of justice and mercy.

Practical Application:

This week, focus on aligning your Sabbath observance with God's call for justice and righteousness.

- **Examine Your Heart:** Reflect on your life and actions. Are there areas where you need to repent and seek God's forgiveness? Pray for a heart that desires to do good and seek justice.
- **Acts of Kindness:** Plan an act of kindness or service for someone in need. This could be helping a neighbor, volunteering, or supporting a cause that promotes justice.
- **Prayer for Justice:** Spend time praying for justice and righteousness in your community and the world. Ask God to show you how you can be an instrument of His Peace and justice.

Prayer:

"Lord, forgive me for any empty rituals and help me to worship You in spirit and truth. Teach me to align my actions with Your will, seeking justice and showing mercy. May my Sabbath observance be pleasing to You as I strive to honor You with my heart and actions. In Jesus' name, Amen."

Sabbath Practice:

Incorporate acts of justice and mercy into your Sabbath observance.

- **Service Project:** Plan a small service project you can do on the Sabbath, such as helping a neighbor or supporting a local charity.
- **Justice Reflection:** Reflect on areas of injustice in your community or the world. Write down ways to make a difference and commit to praying for those affected.

Reflect and Renew:

True Sabbath worship goes beyond rituals to a heart that seeks to do God's will. As you observe the Sabbath this week, focus on aligning your actions with God's call for justice and righteousness. Let your worship be genuine and pleasing to God.

Week 15: A Day for Worship

Scripture Verse:

Leviticus 23:3 (ESV) - "Six days shall work be done, but on the seventh day is a Sabbath of solemn rest, a holy convocation. You shall do no work. It is a Sabbath to the LORD in all your dwelling places."

Reflection:

Leviticus 23:3 establishes the Sabbath as a day of solemn rest and a holy convocation, a time set apart for gathering and worshiping God. The Sabbath is a day of physical rest, communal worship, and spiritual renewal. It is a day to come together with others to celebrate God's goodness, hear His Word, and encourage one another in faith.

The concept of a holy convocation emphasizes the importance of community in our spiritual lives. Gathering with other believers on the Sabbath strengthens our faith, provides mutual encouragement, and allows us to worship God collectively. It reminds us that we are part of a larger family of faith and that our worship is enhanced when we join.

Practical Application:

This week, focus on making the Sabbath a day for communal worship and fellowship.

- **Attend Worship Services:** Make attending a worship service a priority on the Sabbath. Engage fully in the service, singing, praying, and listening to the sermon.
- **Fellowship with Believers:** Spend time with fellow believers outside the formal service. This could include a meal, a small group meeting, or simply enjoying each other's company.
- **Encourage One Another:** Find ways to encourage and uplift others in your faith community. Share what God has been doing in your life, and listen to others' experiences.

Prayer:

"Lord, thank You for the gift of the Sabbath and the opportunity to gather with other believers. Please help me prioritize communal worship and fellowship during the Sabbath. Strengthen my faith as I join others in praising You and hearing Your Word. May our gatherings be a time of encouragement and spiritual renewal. In Jesus' name, Amen."

Sabbath Practice:

Make communal worship and fellowship a central part of your Sabbath observance.

- **Host a Gathering:** If possible, host a gathering for friends or family on the Sabbath. Share a meal, worship together, and discuss how God has worked in your lives.
- **Participate Actively:** Engage actively in your church's Sabbath worship service. Sing enthusiastically, pray sincerely, and listen attentively to the message.

Reflect and Renew:

The Sabbath is a day for worship and community. As you observe the Sabbath this week, embrace the opportunity to gather with other believers and to worship God together. Let your communal worship strengthen your faith and renew your spirit.

Week 16: The Joy of the Sabbath

Scripture Verse:

Nehemiah 8:10-12 (ESV) - "Then he said to them, 'Go your way. Eat the fat, drink sweet wine, and send portions to anyone with nothing ready, for this day is holy to our Lord. And do not be grieved, for the joy of the LORD is your strength.' So the Levites calmed all the people, saying, 'Be quiet, for this day is holy; do not be grieved.' And all the people went their way to eat, drink, send portions, and have great rejoicing because they had understood the words declared to them."

Reflection:

In Nehemiah 8, the people of Israel rediscover the joy of the Lord as they gather to hear the reading of the Law. Despite their initial sorrow over their sins, they are encouraged to celebrate and find strength in the joy of the Lord. The Sabbath, as a holy day, is an opportunity to experience this joy and to celebrate God's goodness.

The joy of the Sabbath comes from understanding and embracing God's Word, spending time in worship, and sharing in fellowship and feasting. It is a day to set aside sorrows and to focus on the blessings and joy that come from knowing God. The joy of the Lord becomes our strength, renewing us and filling us with hope and gladness.

Practical Application:

This week, focus on experiencing and sharing the joy of the Sabbath.

- **Celebrate with Joy:** Plan a joyful Sabbath celebration. Prepare a special meal, invite friends or family, and rejoice in God's blessings.
- **Share with Others:** Follow Nehemiah's example by sharing with those who have less. Invite someone who may be lonely or in need to join your celebration.
- **Reflect on God's Goodness:** Reflect on how God has blessed you. Write down these blessings and thank God for His goodness.

Prayer:

"Lord, thank You for the joy of knowing and understanding Your Word. Help me embrace the Sabbath's joy and celebrate Your goodness. Fill my heart with gratitude and gladness, and may Your joy be my strength. In Jesus' name, Amen."

Sabbath Practice:

Make joy a central theme of your Sabbath observance.

- **Joyful Feasting:** Prepare a special meal you can enjoy with loved ones. Use this time to celebrate and give thanks for God's blessings.
- **Acts of Joy:** Engage in activities that bring you joy and laughter. This could be playing games, enjoying a hobby, or spending time in nature.

Reflect and Renew:

The Sabbath is a day to experience and share the joy of the Lord. As you observe the Sabbath this week, focus on celebrating God's goodness and sharing that joy with others. Let the joy of the Lord be your strength and fill your heart with gladness.

Summary of April: The Sabbath as Worship

The theme for April is "The Sabbath as Worship." Throughout this month, we have explored how the Sabbath is a day of rest and dedicated time to worship God. Each week, we focused on different aspects of worship and how they enrich our observance of the Sabbath.

Reflecting on the Month

AS YOU REFLECT ON THE past month, consider how your understanding of the Sabbath as a time for worship has deepened. How has focusing on prayer, justice, community, and joy transformed your Sabbath observance? Have you experienced a greater sense of connection with God and others?

- **Personal Reflections:** Spend time journaling about your experiences this month. What have you learned about worship on the Sabbath? How have these insights changed your approach to the day?
- **Gratitude:** Reflect on how worship has renewed your life and joy. Write down the blessings you have experienced, and thank God for His goodness.

Invitation to Continue the Journey

The journey of worshiping God on the Sabbath is ongoing. As you move forward, carry the lessons and practices you have developed this month. Continue to seek God's presence, align your actions with His values, engage in communal worship, and celebrate His blessings with joy.

- **Ongoing Practice:** Make worship an integral part of your Sabbath observance. Focus on honoring God through your actions, fellowship, and joyful celebrations.
- **Community Sharing:** Share your insights and experiences with your faith community. Encourage others to embrace the Sabbath as a time for worship and renewal.

May the foundation you have built this month continue to support and enrich your journey throughout the year. Embrace each Sabbath with a renewed sense of purpose, joy, and connection with God. Let His teachings and example guide you into deeper worship and peace.

Looking Ahead

As you prepare to move into the next month of "The 7th Day" devotional, look forward to exploring new themes and insights about the Sabbath. Each month builds upon the previous one, offering a more profound understanding of rest and renewal. May you be blessed as you continue this journey, finding ever deeper worship and joy in the gift of the Sabbath.

May: Finding Peace in Rest

Week 17: Peace in God's Presence

Scripture Verse:

John 14:27 (ESV) - Peace I leave with you; my peace I give to you. Not as the world gives do I give to you. Let not your hearts be troubled, neither let them be afraid."

Reflection:

In John 14:27, Jesus offers His disciples a profound gift—His Peace. This peace is unlike anything the world can give. A deep, abiding peace calms our fears and soothes our troubled hearts. Jesus' peace sustains us through life's challenges and uncertainties.

The Sabbath is a perfect opportunity to embrace this peace. By setting aside time to rest and focus on God's presence, we open our hearts to receive the Peace Jesus offers. This peace is not dependent on our circumstances but is rooted in our relationship with Him. As we spend time in His presence, we are reminded that He is in control and that we can trust Him with our worries and fears.

Practical Application:

This week, focus on experiencing and embracing the Peace of Jesus.

- **Quiet Reflection:** Spend time each day in quiet reflection, meditating on John 14:27. Allow Jesus' words to calm your heart and bring you peace.
- **Peaceful Activities:** Engage in activities that promote peace and relaxation, such as reading a devotional, listening to calming music, or taking a nature walk.
- **Letting Go of Worries:** Write down your worries and fears and pray them to God. Ask Him to replace your anxiety with His Peace.

Prayer:

"Lord Jesus, thank You for the gift of Your Peace. Help me to embrace this peace and to trust You with my worries and fears. May Your Peace fill my heart and calm my soul as I spend time in Your presence. In Your name, Amen."

Sabbath Practice:

Create a Sabbath experience focused on peace and relaxation.

- **Peaceful Environment:** Set up a quiet space in your home where you can relax and reflect. Use calming elements like candles, soft music, and comfortable seating.
- **Peace Walk:** Take a peaceful walk in a natural setting. Use this time to pray, meditate on John 14:27, and absorb the tranquility of God's creation.

Reflect and Renew:

Jesus offers you a peace that surpasses all understanding. As you observe the Sabbath this week, embrace His Peace and let it calm your heart and mind. Rest assured that He is in control, and His Peace is always available to you.

Week 18: Rest for the Soul

Scripture Verse:

Psalm 62:1-2 (ESV) - "For God alone, my soul waits in silence; from him comes my salvation. He alone is my rock, salvation, and fortress; I shall not be greatly shaken."

Reflection:

Psalm 62:1-2 speaks of a deep, soul-refreshing rest from waiting on God in silence. The psalmist recognizes that true rest and salvation come from God alone, our rock and fortress. When we rest in God, we find stability and security that life's challenges cannot shake.

The Sabbath is an ideal time to seek this kind of soul rest. Setting aside time to be still before God allows our souls to be refreshed and renewed. This rest is physical and spiritual, as we find peace and assurance in God's unchanging presence and strength.

Practical Application:

This week, focus on finding rest for your soul by waiting on God in silence and stillness.

- **Silent Meditation:** Set aside time each day for quiet meditation. Wait on God in silence, allowing His presence to fill your heart and mind.
- **Scripture Reflection:** Meditate on Psalm 62:1-2, reflecting on God as your rock and fortress. Let these truths bring you comfort and rest.
- **Soul Refreshment:** Engage in activities that refresh your soul, such as reading Scripture, journaling, or spending time in nature.

Prayer:

"Lord, You are my rock and my salvation. Help me to wait on You in silence and to find rest for my soul in Your presence. Refresh and renew my spirit as I draw near to You. In Jesus' name, Amen."

Sabbath Practice:

Incorporate silent meditation and soul-refreshing activities into your Sabbath observance.

- **Silent Retreat:** Create a mini-retreat at home where you can spend extended time in silence and prayer. Listen to God's voice and rest in His presence.
- **Nature Reflection:** Spend time in a quiet, natural setting, reflecting on God's creation and His steadfast love. Allow the beauty of nature to refresh your soul.

Reflect and Renew:

True rest comes from waiting on God and finding refuge in His presence. As you observe the Sabbath this week, seek soul-refreshing rest by still before God and trusting in His unshakeable strength. Let His presence bring you peace and renewal.

WEEK 19: THE PEACE of Christ

Scripture Verse:

Colossians 3:15 (ESV) - "And let the Peace of Christ rule in your hearts, to which indeed you were called in one body. And be thankful."

Reflection:

In Colossians 3:15, Paul encourages believers to let the Peace of Christ rule in their hearts. This peace is meant to govern our thoughts, emotions, and actions, providing a foundation for unity and gratitude within the body of Christ. When the Peace of Christ rules our hearts, it shapes our interactions with others and influences how we respond to life's challenges.

The Sabbath is a time to invite the Peace of Christ to take control of our hearts. By setting aside time for rest and reflection, we create space for His Peace to fill and guide us. This peace brings personal tranquility and fosters harmony and gratitude in our relationships with others.

Practical Application:

This week, focus on allowing the Peace of Christ to rule your heart and shape your interactions with others.

- **Heart Examination:** Reflect on areas where you need the Peace of Christ to rule. Pray for His Peace to fill those areas and to guide your thoughts and actions.
- **Gratitude Practice:** Cultivate a heart of gratitude by writing down things you are thankful for each day. Let gratitude enhance the peace in your heart.
- **Peaceful Interactions:** Be intentional about fostering peace in your interactions with others. Seek to be a peacemaker in your relationships and to respond with grace and kindness.

Prayer:

"Lord Jesus, let Your peace rule in my heart. Fill me with Your tranquility and guide my thoughts and actions. Please help me cultivate gratitude and be a peacemaker in my relationships. Thank You for calling me to peace and unity in Your body. In Your name, Amen."

Sabbath Practice:

Create a peaceful and grateful atmosphere for your Sabbath observance.

- **Peaceful Environment:** Set up a quiet space for your Sabbath, using calming elements like soft lighting, soothing music, and comfortable seating.
- **Gratitude Journal:** Start a gratitude journal for the Sabbath. Write down things you are thankful for and reflect on how Christ's Peace has influenced your week.

Reflect and Renew:

The Peace of Christ is a powerful force that can transform your heart and relationships. As you observe the Sabbath this week, invite His Peace to rule in your heart and guide your actions. Let this peace foster gratitude and harmony, bringing you closer to God and others.

Week 20: Casting Cares on Him

Scripture Verse:

1 Peter 5:7 (ESV) - "Casting all your anxieties on him, because he cares for you."

Reflection:

1 Peter 5:7 offers a comforting promise: we can cast all our anxieties on God because He cares for us. This verse invites us to release our worries and burdens to Him, trusting in His loving care and provision. Holding onto anxiety can weigh us down, but giving our concerns to God brings freedom and peace.

The Sabbath is an ideal time to practice casting our cares on God. By intentionally setting aside our worries and focusing on His care, we can experience deeper rest and renewal. This trust brings peace and strengthens our relationship with God as we rely on His faithfulness.

Practical Application:

This week, focus on casting your anxieties on God and trusting His care.

- **Anxiety List:** Write down your anxieties and concerns. Bring this list to God in prayer, asking Him to take each worry and to provide peace and resolution.
- **Trust Practice:** Throughout the week, whenever you feel anxious, remind yourself of 1 Peter 5:7. Consciously cast your anxiety on God and trust in His care.
- **Prayer Support:** Share your burdens with a trusted friend or family member and ask them to pray for you. Sometimes, sharing our worries with others can help us feel supported and cared for.

Prayer:
"Lord, thank You for inviting me to cast my anxieties on You. Help me trust in Your care and release my worries into Your hands. May I find peace and rest in Your loving provision. In Jesus' name, Amen."

Sabbath Practice:
Dedicate part of your Sabbath to casting your cares on God and experiencing His Peace.

- **Care Release Ritual:** Create a ritual for releasing your anxieties. This could include writing your worries on paper and placing them in a "God box" or burning them as a symbol of letting go.
- **Peaceful Meditation:** Spend quiet meditation, focusing on God's care for you. Use deep breathing exercises to help release tension and foster a sense of calm.

Reflect and Renew:
God cares deeply for you and invites you to cast all your anxieties on Him. As you observe the Sabbath this week, release your worries into His loving hands. Trust in His care and provision, and let His Peace fill your heart and mind. Through this practice, you will find greater rest and renewal in His presence.

Summary of May: Finding Peace in Rest

The theme for May is "Finding Peace in Rest." This month, we have focused on embracing the Peace God offers us through the Sabbath. We explored different aspects of experiencing and maintaining peace each week, learning to cast our anxieties on God and finding rest for our souls.

Reflecting on the Month

As you reflect on the past month, consider how embracing the Peace of God has impacted your life. How has focusing on peace during the Sabbath brought rest and renewal to your spirit? Have you experienced a deeper trust in God's care and provision?

- **Personal Reflections:** Spend time journaling about your experiences this month. What have you learned about finding peace in rest? How have these insights changed your approach to the Sabbath?
- **Gratitude:** Reflect on the ways God's Peace has blessed you. Write down the moments when you felt His Peace most profoundly and thank Him for His care.

Invitation to Continue the Journey

The journey of finding peace in rest is ongoing. As you move forward, carry the lessons and practices you have developed this month. Continue to seek God's presence, embrace His Peace, and cast your anxieties on Him.

- **Ongoing Practice:** Make peace a central theme of your Sabbath observance. Keep focusing on practices that bring rest and renewal.

- **Community Sharing:** Share your insights and experiences with your faith community. Encourage others to embrace the Peace that God offers through the Sabbath.

May the foundation you have built this month continue to support and enrich your journey throughout the year. Embrace each Sabbath with renewed peace and trust in God's care. Let His peace guide you into deeper rest and renewal.

Looking Ahead

As you prepare to move into the next month of "The 7th Day" devotional, look forward to exploring new themes and insights about the Sabbath. Each month builds upon the previous one, offering a more profound understanding of rest and renewal.

In June, we will focus on "The Rhythm of Rest," exploring how to balance work and rest in our daily lives. We will examine establishing a healthy rhythm that honors God's design for rest and work. May you be blessed as you continue this journey, finding ever deeper peace and joy in the gift of the Sabbath.

June: The Rhythm of Rest

Week 21: Work and Rest Balance

Scripture Verse:

Exodus 34:21 (ESV) - "Six days you shall work, but on the seventh day you shall rest. In plowing time and harvest, you shall rest."

Reflection:

Exodus 34:21 emphasizes the balance between work and rest. Even during the busiest times of the year, such as plowing and harvest, God commands His people to rest on the seventh day. This balance is essential for our well-being, reminding us that rest is not optional but a necessary part of life.

Balancing work and rest is vital in today's fast-paced world. Constant work without rest leads to burnout and stress, while regular rest rejuvenates our bodies and minds. The Sabbath provides a structured time to cease our labors and find refreshment in God's presence, allowing us to return to our work with renewed energy and perspective.

Practical Application:

This week, focus on establishing a healthy balance between work and rest.

- **Schedule Rest:** Intentionally schedule rest periods throughout your week. Ensure you set aside the Sabbath as a dedicated day of rest.
- **Evaluate Workload:** Assess your current workload and identify areas where you can delegate or reduce tasks. Create a balanced schedule that allows time for both work and rest.
- **Rest Activities:** Plan restful activities for the Sabbath that help you relax and recharge. This could include spending time with family, reading, or enjoying nature.

Prayer:

"Lord, thank You for teaching us the importance of balancing work and rest. Help me honor the Sabbath and find a healthy rhythm in my daily life. Give me the wisdom to manage my workload and to prioritize rest as You command. In Jesus' name, Amen."

Sabbath Practice:

Create a balanced Sabbath experience that includes restful activities and time with God.

- **Restful Routine:** Establish a restful routine for the Sabbath, including activities that help you relax and enjoy God's presence.
- **Family Time:** Spend quality time with your family, engaging in activities that strengthen your relationships and bring joy.

Reflect and Renew:

Balancing work and rest is essential for a healthy and fulfilling life. As you observe the Sabbath this week, focus on creating a rhythm that honors your need for work and rest. Let this balance bring you closer to God and renew your spirit.

Week 22: Daily Rest in God

Scripture Verse:

Matthew 6:25-34 (ESV) - "Therefore I tell you, do not be anxious about your life, what you will eat or drink, nor about your body, what you will put on. Is not life more than food and the body more than clothing? Look at the birds of the air: they neither sow nor reap nor gather into barns, yet your heavenly Father feeds them. Are you not of more value than they? And which of you, by being anxious, can add a single hour to his life span? And why are you anxious about clothing? Consider the lilies of the field, how they grow: they neither toil nor spin, yet I tell you, even Solomon in all his glory was not arrayed like one of these. But if God so clothes the grass of the field, which today is alive and tomorrow is thrown into the oven, will he not much more clothe you, O you of little faith? Therefore, do not be anxious, saying, 'What shall we eat?' or 'What shall we drink?' or 'What shall we wear?' For the Gentiles seek after all these things, and your heavenly Father knows that you need them all. But seek first the kingdom of God and his righteousness, and all these things will be added to you."

Reflection:

In Matthew 6:25-34, Jesus addresses the worries and anxieties that often plague our daily lives. He encourages us to trust God's provision and prioritize seeking His kingdom and righteousness. This passage reminds us that God cares for all our needs and that we can find daily rest in His faithfulness.

Daily rest in God involves letting go of our anxieties and trusting in His care. It means finding peace knowing God values us and will provide for our needs. Focusing on God's kingdom and righteousness can shift our perspective from our worries to His promises.

Practical Application:

This week, focus on finding daily rest in God by releasing your anxieties and trusting His provision.

- **Daily Devotion:** Spend time each day in prayer and reading Scripture, focusing on God's promises and His care for you.
- **Trust Practice:** Whenever you feel anxious, remind yourself of Matthew 6:25-34. Consciously choose to trust God and release your worries to Him.
- **Gratitude Journal:** Keep a gratitude journal, writing down the ways God has provided for you each day. This practice will reinforce your trust in His faithfulness.

Prayer:

"Lord, thank You for Your promise to provide for all my needs. Help me to trust You more and to release my anxieties into Your loving hands. May I rest daily in Your faithfulness and seek Your kingdom above all else. In Jesus' name, Amen."

Sabbath Practice:

Incorporate practices that reinforce trust and gratitude into your Sabbath observance.

- **Nature Reflection:** Spend time in nature, reflecting on God's care for His creation and provision for you. Let the beauty of creation remind you of His faithfulness.
- **Trust Ritual:** Create a simple ritual for releasing your worries, such as writing them down and placing them in a "God box" to symbolize entrusting them to Him.

Reflect and Renew:

Finding daily rest in God involves trusting His provision and releasing our anxieties. As you observe the Sabbath this week, focus on deepening your trust in God and finding peace in His faithfulness. Let this trust bring you daily rest and renewal.

Week 23: Weekly Sabbath

Scripture Verse:

Leviticus 25:4 (ESV) - "But in the seventh year there shall be a Sabbath of solemn rest for the land, a Sabbath to the LORD. You shall not sow your field or prune your vineyard."

Reflection:

Leviticus 25:4 introduces the concept of a sabbatical year when the land is given a rest from agricultural activities. This extended Sabbath emphasizes the importance of rest for individuals and the entire creation. It also underscores the principle that everything, including the land, needs a time of renewal and restoration.

The weekly Sabbath serves as a regular reminder of this principle. By observing a day of rest each week, we align ourselves with God's rhythm of work and rest. This weekly Sabbath provides a consistent opportunity to step back from our labors, reconnect with God, and find renewal for the days ahead.

Practical Application:

This week, focus on observing the weekly Sabbath as a time for renewal and restoration.

- **Plan Ahead:** Prepare for the Sabbath by completing necessary tasks ahead of time. This will help you fully embrace the day of rest without distractions.
- **Sabbath Rituals:** Establish rituals that help you transition into the Sabbath, such as lighting candles, playing soothing music, or reading a favorite Scripture passage.
- **Restful Activities:** Plan activities that help you relax and recharge, such as spending time with family, enjoying a hobby, or taking a leisurely walk.

Prayer:

"Lord, thank You for the gift of the Sabbath and the reminder to rest and renew. Help me honor this day and find true rest in Your presence. May my Sabbath observance bring me closer to You and refresh my spirit for the week ahead. In Jesus' name, Amen."

Sabbath Practice:

Create a meaningful Sabbath experience with rituals and activities that promote rest and renewal.

- **Sabbath Meal:** Prepare a special meal to enjoy with loved ones. Use this time to connect, share, and celebrate the Sabbath together.
- **Reflection Time:** Set aside time for personal reflection and prayer. Write down your thoughts, prayers, and insights from the week in a journal.

Reflect and Renew:

The weekly Sabbath is a gift of rest and renewal. As you observe the Sabbath this week, embrace the opportunity to step back from your labors and find refreshment in God's presence. Let this rest time prepare you for the days ahead and deepen your relationship with God.

Week 24: Annual Sabbath Rest

Scripture Verse:

Leviticus 25:8-12 (ESV) - "You shall count seven weeks of years, seven times seven years so that the time of the seven weeks of years shall give you forty-nine years. Then, you shall sound the loud trumpet on the tenth day of the seventh month. On the Day of Atonement, you shall sound the trumpet throughout all your land. And you shall consecrate the fiftieth year and proclaim liberty throughout the land to all its inhabitants. It shall be a jubilee for you when each of you returns to his property and his clan. That fiftieth year shall be a jubilee for you; in it, you shall neither sow nor reap nor gather what grows of itself nor the grapes from the undressed vines, for it is a jubilee. It shall be holy to you. You may eat the produce of the field."

Reflection:

The concept of the Jubilee year, introduced in Leviticus 25, emphasizes a profound rest and renewal not just for individuals but for the entire community and land. Every fiftieth year, debts were forgiven, slaves were freed, and the land itself was given a rest from agricultural activities. This practice underscores God's desire for comprehensive renewal and restoration, impacting every aspect of life.

The Jubilee year is a powerful reminder that God values rest, freedom, and restoration. It teaches us the importance of periodic, extended rest and the need to release and reset our lives. This kind of rest allows us to experience God's provision profoundly and trust in His timing and care.

Practical Application:

This week, focus on the concept of extended rest and renewal. Consider incorporating periods of deeper rest and restoration into your life.

- **Plan for Rest:** Reflect on your yearly schedule and identify when you can take extended breaks for rest and renewal. This might include vacations, retreats, or sabbaticals.
- **Practice Forgiveness:** Just as the Jubilee year involved forgiving debts, consider ways to practice forgiveness and release in your life. Let go of grudges and extend grace to others.
- **Community Care:** Think about how you can contribute to the renewal and restoration of your community. This could involve volunteering, supporting local initiatives, or helping those in need.

Prayer:

"Lord, thank You for the concept of the Jubilee year and the reminder of the importance of rest and renewal. Please help me incorporate extended rest periods into my life and practice forgiveness and grace. Guide me in contributing to my community's renewal and trusting Your provision and care. In Jesus' name, Amen."

Sabbath Practice:

Incorporate elements of the Jubilee into your Sabbath observance this week.

- **Extended Reflection:** Dedicate a longer period for reflection and prayer. Use this time to think about areas that need renewal and restoration.
- **Act of Kindness:** Perform an act of kindness or service for someone in your community. This could be helping a neighbor, volunteering, or supporting someone in need.

Reflect and Renew:

The Jubilee year emphasizes the importance of comprehensive rest and renewal. As you observe the Sabbath this week, consider incorporating extended rest periods. Embrace the principles of forgiveness and community care, trust in God's provision, and experience His profound peace and renewal.

Summary of June: The Rhythm of Rest

The theme for June is "The Rhythm of Rest." Throughout this month, we have focused on establishing a healthy balance between work and rest, both in our daily lives and through the observance of the Sabbath. Each week, we explored different aspects of finding rest in God and creating a rhythm that honors His design for rest and work.

Reflecting on the Month

As you reflect on the past month, consider how establishing a rhythm of rest has impacted your life. How has focusing on balancing work and rest, trusting in God's provision, and embracing the Sabbath brought renewal and restoration to your spirit? Have you experienced a deeper sense of peace and connection with God?

- **Personal Reflections:** Spend time journaling about your experiences this month. What have you learned about the rhythm of rest? How have these insights changed your approach to work and rest?
- **Gratitude:** Reflect on how God's rhythm of rest has blessed you. Write down the moments when you felt the most refreshed and thank Him for His guidance.

INVITATION TO CONTINUE the Journey

Establishing a rhythm of rest is an ongoing journey. As you move forward, carry the lessons and practices you have developed this month. Continue to seek a balanced rhythm in your daily life, trusting in God's provision and finding renewal through the Sabbath.

- **Ongoing Practice:** Make rest a regular part of your routine. Keep focusing on balancing work and rest, practicing daily trust, and intentionally observing the Sabbath.
- **Community Sharing:** Share your insights and experiences with your faith community. Encourage others to embrace the rhythm of rest and to find renewal in God's design for rest and work.

May the foundation you have built this month continue to support and enrich your journey throughout the year. Embrace each day and each Sabbath with a renewed sense of balance, peace, and connection with God. Let His rhythm of rest guide you into deeper renewal and fulfillment.

Looking Ahead

As you prepare to move into the next month of "The 7th Day" devotional, look forward to exploring new themes and insights about the Sabbath. Each month builds upon the previous one, offering a more profound understanding of rest and renewal.

In July, we will focus on "Rest in God's Creation," exploring how engaging with nature and appreciating God's creation can bring rest and renewal to our lives. May you be blessed as you continue this journey, finding ever deeper peace and joy in the gift of the Sabbath.

July: Rest in God's Creation

Week 25: The Beauty of Creation

Scripture Verse:

Psalm 19:1-6 (ESV) - "The heavens declare the glory of God, and the sky above proclaims his handiwork. Day-to-day pours out speech, and night-to-night reveals knowledge. There is no speech or words, whose voice is not heard. Their voice goes through all the earth, and their words to the end of the world. In them he has set a tent for the sun, which comes out like a bridegroom leaving his chamber and, like a strong man, runs its course with joy. Its rising is from the end of the heavens, and its circuit to the end of them, and there is nothing hidden from its heat."

Reflection:

Psalm 19 beautifully illustrates how creation itself declares the glory of God. The heavens, the sky, and all of nature speak of God's handiwork without words, revealing His power and majesty. This passage encourages us to look at the world around us and see the evidence of God's creativity and care in every detail of creation.

The beauty of creation is a testament to God's greatness and a reminder of His presence in our lives. By observing and appreciating the natural world, we can find rest and renewal, reconnecting with God in a profound way. Nature can calm our spirits and remind us of the bigger picture, drawing our hearts towards worship.

Practical Application:

This week, focus on appreciating the beauty of creation and seeing it as a declaration of God's glory.

- **Nature Walk:** Walk in a park, forest, or natural setting. Pay attention to the details around you, such as the colors, sounds, and textures. Reflect on how these elements display God's creativity.
- **Photography:** Capture the beauty of creation through photography. Take pictures of landscapes, flowers, animals, or anything that catches your eye. Use these images as a reminder of God's handiwork.
- **Sky Gazing:** Spend time observing the sky during the day and night. Notice the clouds' patterns, the sun's movement, and the stars. Let these observations lead you to praise God for His magnificent creation.

Prayer:

"Lord, thank You for the beauty of creation that declares Your glory. Help me appreciate the world and see Your handiwork in every detail. May the beauty of creation draw my heart towards worship and remind me of Your greatness. In Jesus' name, Amen."

Sabbath Practice:

Dedicate part of your Sabbath to experiencing and reflecting on the beauty of creation.

- **Outdoor Reflection:** Spend part of your Sabbath outdoors, in a natural setting. Bring a journal and write down your reflections on how nature speaks of God's glory.
- **Creation Art:** Engage in a creative activity that celebrates the beauty of creation, such as painting, drawing, or crafting. Use this time to meditate on God's handiwork and express your gratitude through art.

Reflect and Renew:

The beauty of creation is a powerful testimony of God's glory and creativity. As you observe the Sabbath this week, appreciate the natural world and let it draw you closer to God. Allow the beauty of creation to bring rest and renewal to your spirit.

Week 26: Sabbath and Creation

Scripture Verse:

Genesis 1:31-2:3 (ESV) - "And God saw everything that he had made, and behold, it was very good. And there was evening, and there was morning, the sixth day. Thus, the heavens and the earth were finished, and all the hosts of them. And on the seventh day God finished his work that he had done, and he rested on the seventh day from all his work that he had done. So God blessed the seventh day and made it holy because on it God rested from all his work that he had done in creation."

Reflection:

The account of creation in Genesis culminates with God resting on the seventh day, declaring everything He had made as "very good." This passage highlights the importance of rest in the rhythm of creation. God's rest was not out of necessity but as a model for us to follow, emphasizing the significance of ceasing our labors and appreciating His work.

The Sabbath is a time to reflect on God's creation and to rest in His completed work. It is a day set apart for us to pause, enjoy, and acknowledge the goodness of what God has made. By observing the Sabbath, we honor God's design and recognize the value of rest and reflection in our lives.

Practical Application:

This week, focus on the connection between the Sabbath and creation. Reflect on how resting on the Sabbath allows you to appreciate and enjoy God's work.

- **Creation Reflection:** Spend time each day reflecting on different aspects of creation. Consider the diversity of life, the intricacies of ecosystems, and the beauty of landscapes.
- **Sabbath Rest:** Plan a restful Sabbath that includes activities that help you appreciate creation, such as hiking, gardening, or simply sitting outside and enjoying nature.
- **Creation Care:** Consider ways you can care for God's creation. These could include recycling, conserving water, or participating in a community clean-up project.

Prayer:

"Lord, thank You for the gift of creation and the example of rest that You set on the seventh day. Help me to honor the Sabbath by resting and reflecting on the goodness of Your creation. May I find renewal and joy as I appreciate the world You have made. In Jesus' name, Amen."

Sabbath Practice:

Dedicate your Sabbath to activities that help you appreciate and reflect on God's creation.

- **Nature Outing:** Plan an outing to a natural area where you can enjoy and reflect on the beauty of creation. Bring a journal or sketchbook to capture your thoughts and observations.
- **Creation Meditation:** Spend time meditating on Genesis 1:31-2:3. Reflect on the significance of God resting and the goodness of His creation. Use this time to pray and thank God for His work.

Reflect and Renew:

The Sabbath is a time to rest and reflect on God's creation. As you observe the Sabbath this week, take time to appreciate the goodness of what God has made and to find rest in His completed work. Let this reflection bring you closer to God and deepen your appreciation for His creation.

Week 27: Enjoying God's Creation

Scripture Verse:

Psalm 104:24-30 (ESV) - "O LORD, how manifold are your works! In wisdom have you made them all; the earth is full of your creatures. Here is the sea, great and wide, which teems with innumerable creatures, living things both small and great. There go the ships and Leviathan, which you formed to play in. These all look to you to give them their food in due season. When you give it to them, they gather it up; when you open your hand, they are filled with good things. When you hide your face, they are dismayed; when you take away their breath, they die and return to their dust. When you send forth your Spirit, they are created, and you renew the face of the ground."

Reflection:

Psalm 104 is a hymn of praise that marvels at the diversity and intricacy of God's creation. The psalmist reflects on God's manifold works, the wisdom with which He has made them, and the dependence of all creatures on His provision. This passage encourages us to enjoy the abundance and variety of life that fills the earth.

Enjoying God's creation is an act of worship. It is a way to recognize His wisdom, creativity, and provision. By taking time to observe and delight in the natural world, we draw closer to the Creator and find a deeper appreciation for His work. This enjoyment also brings rest and renewal to our spirits as we reconnect with the beauty and wonder of God's creation.

Practical Application:

This week, focus on enjoying the diversity and beauty of God's creation. Take time to observe, appreciate, and delight in the natural world.

- **Wildlife Observation:** Spend time observing wildlife in your area. This could be birds, insects, animals, or marine life. Reflect on the variety and intricacy of God's creatures.
- **Creative Expression:** Use art, photography, or writing to capture and express the beauty of creation. Share your creations with others to inspire appreciation for God's work.
- **Nature Activities:** Engage in activities that allow you to enjoy nature, such as hiking, swimming, or stargazing. Use these moments to thank God for the beauty and diversity of His creation.

Prayer:

"Lord, how manifold are Your works! In wisdom, You have made them all. Help me to take joy in Your creation and appreciate the natural world's diversity and beauty. May my enjoyment of creation draw me closer to You and inspire gratitude and wonder in my heart. In Jesus' name, Amen."

Sabbath Practice:

Dedicate part of your Sabbath to enjoying and delighting in God's creation.

- **Nature Adventure:** Plan a nature adventure, such as a hike, a visit to the beach, or a picnic in the park. Take time to observe and appreciate the details of the natural world.
- **Creative Sabbath:** Use your creative talents to express your appreciation for creation. Draw, paint, write, or photograph aspects of nature that inspire you.

Reflect and Renew:

Enjoying God's creation is a way to worship and connect with the Creator. As you observe the Sabbath this week, take time to delight in the diversity and beauty of the natural world. Let your enjoyment of creation bring you closer to God and fill your heart with gratitude and wonder.

Week 28: Stewardship and Rest

Scripture Verse:

Genesis 2:15 (ESV) - "The LORD God took the man and put him in the garden of Eden to work it and keep it."

Reflection:

Genesis 2:15 highlights humanity's role as stewards of God's creation. God placed Adam in the Garden of Eden to work it and keep it, indicating that caring for creation is a significant responsibility. Stewardship involves cultivating and preserving the natural world, ensuring it remains healthy and productive for future generations.

Rest and stewardship are closely connected. By observing the Sabbath and taking time to rest, we acknowledge our dependence on God and our role as caretakers of His creation. Resting allows us to reflect on our stewardship responsibilities and renew our commitment to environmental care. It also provides an opportunity to practice sustainable habits contributing to the earth's well-being.

Practical Application:

This week, focus on your role as a steward of God's creation. Reflect on how you can care for the environment and practice sustainable habits.

- **Sustainable Practices:** Implement sustainable practices in your daily life, such as recycling, conserving water, reducing waste, and using energy-efficient products.
- **Community Involvement:** Participate in community efforts to care for the environment, such as local clean-up projects, tree planting, or conservation initiatives.
- **Educational Growth:** Educate yourself about environmental issues and how you can make a positive impact. Share this knowledge with others to promote awareness and action.

Prayer:

"Lord, thank You for entrusting me with the responsibility of caring for Your creation. Help me to be a faithful steward and to practice sustainable habits that honor You. As I rest and reflect on the Sabbath, renew my commitment to caring for the environment and living in harmony with Your creation. In Jesus' name, Amen."

Sabbath Practice:

Incorporate activities that promote stewardship and reflection into your Sabbath observance.

- **Nature Care:** Spend part of your Sabbath caring for a local natural area, such as a park, garden, or beach. This could involve picking up litter, planting trees, or tending to plants.
- **Sustainable Sabbath:** Practice a sustainable Sabbath by minimizing waste, conserving resources, and using eco-friendly products. Reflect on how these practices contribute to the well-being of creation.

Reflect and Renew:

Stewardship and rest go hand in hand. As you observe the Sabbath this week, reflect on your role as a caretaker of God's creation and commit to practicing sustainable habits. Let your rest renew your commitment to stewardship and deepen your appreciation for the environment. By caring for creation, you honor God and contribute to the flourishing of the world He has made.

Summary of July: Rest in God's Creation

The theme for July is "Rest in God's Creation." Throughout this month, we have focused on the beauty, enjoyment, and stewardship of God's creation, learning how engaging with nature can bring rest and renewal to our lives. We explored different aspects of experiencing and appreciating creation and our responsibility to care for it each week.

REFLECTING ON THE MONTH

As you reflect on the past month, consider how engaging with God's creation has impacted your life. How has focusing on creation's beauty, enjoyment, and stewardship brought rest and renewal to your spirit? Have you experienced a deeper sense of connection with God through nature?

- **Personal Reflections:** Spend time journaling about your experiences this month. What have you learned about resting in God's creation? How have these insights changed your approach to the Sabbath and daily life?
- **Gratitude:** Reflect on the moments when you felt most connected to God through nature. Write down these experiences and thank Him for the beauty and diversity of His creation.

Invitation to Continue the Journey

The journey of resting in God's creation is ongoing. As you move forward, carry the lessons and practices you have developed this month. Continue to seek opportunities to engage with nature, appreciate its beauty, and practice stewardship.

- **Ongoing Practice:** Make time for nature a regular part of your routine. Keep focusing on activities that allow you to enjoy and care for creation.
- **Community Sharing:** Share your insights and experiences with your faith community. Encourage others to find rest and renewal in God's creation.

May the foundation you have built this month continue to support and enrich your journey throughout the year. Embrace each day and each Sabbath with a renewed sense of wonder and gratitude for God's creation. Let His handiwork draw you closer to Him and inspire you to live in harmony with the world He has made.

Looking Ahead

As you prepare to move into the next month of "The 7th Day" devotional, look forward to exploring new themes and insights about the Sabbath. Each month builds upon the previous one, offering a more profound understanding of rest and renewal.

In August, we will focus on "Spiritual Renewal through Rest," exploring how prayer, meditation, and fasting can deepen our connection with God and bring spiritual refreshment. May you be blessed as you continue this journey, finding ever deeper peace and joy in the gift of the Sabbath.

August: Spiritual Renewal through Rest

Week 29: Renewal in God's Word

Scripture Verse:

Psalm 119:114-117 (ESV) - "You are my hiding place and my shield; I hope in your word. Depart from me, you evildoers, that I may keep the commandments of my God. Uphold me according to your promise that I may live, and let me not be put to shame in my hope! Hold me up, that I may be safe and have regard for your statutes continually!"

Reflection:

Psalm 119 emphasizes the importance of God's Word as a source of hope, protection, and renewal. The psalmist finds refuge in God's Word, viewing it as a hiding place and a shield against life's challenges. Immersing ourselves in Scripture provides guidance, comfort, and strength.

Renewal in God's Word involves more than just reading; it means allowing the truths of Scripture to penetrate our hearts and transform our lives. Our faith upholds and strengthens us as we meditate on God's promises and commandments. The Sabbath is an ideal time to dive deeper into the Bible and let it renew our spirits.

Practical Application:

This week, focus on finding renewal in God's Word by incorporating it more deeply into your Sabbath observance.

- **Daily Reading:** Set aside time daily to read and meditate on Scripture. Choose passages that speak to your current circumstances and reflect on their meaning.
- **Scripture Memorization:** Memorize key verses from Psalm 119:114-117. Repeat them daily to remind yourself of God's promises and protection.
- **Bible Study:** Dedicate a portion of your Sabbath to in-depth Bible study. Use commentaries, study guides, or group discussions to enhance your understanding of the passages.

Prayer:

"Lord, thank You for Your Word, a source of hope and renewal. Help me to immerse myself in Scripture and to allow Your promises to uphold and strengthen me. May Your Word be my hiding place and shield, guiding me in all aspects of my life. In Jesus' name, Amen."

Sabbath Practice:

Incorporate extended time in God's Word into your Sabbath observance.

- **Quiet Time:** Create a quiet, comfortable space for reading and meditating on Scripture. Use this time to reflect on God's promises and how they apply to your life.
- **Journaling:** Write down insights and reflections from your Bible reading. Keep a journal to record how God's Word speaks to you and transforms your heart.

Reflect and Renew:

God's Word is a powerful source of renewal and strength. As you observe the Sabbath this week, dedicate time to immerse yourself in Scripture and let its truths refresh your spirit. Find refuge and hope in God's promises, allowing His Word to guide and uphold you.

Week 30: Spiritual Refreshment

Scripture Verse:

Isaiah 40:29-31 (ESV) - "He gives power to the faint, and to him who has no might he increases strength. Even youths shall faint and be weary, and young men shall fall exhausted, but they who wait for the LORD shall renew their strength; they shall mount up with wings like eagles; they shall run and not be weary; they shall walk and not faint."

Reflection:

Isaiah 40:29-31 highlights God's promise to renew the strength of those waiting for Him. Even the strongest among us can grow weary, but God offers a profound refreshment and renewal to those who trust Him. This passage assures us that when we rely on God, we can find the strength to rise above our challenges and continue our journey with renewed energy.

Spiritual refreshment comes from waiting on the Lord and trusting His power and timing. The Sabbath provides a special opportunity to pause, wait on God, and receive the renewal He promises. By resting in His presence, we can experience a deep rejuvenation that enables us to face life's demands with renewed vigor.

Practical Application:

This week, focus on finding spiritual refreshment by waiting on the Lord and trusting His strength.

- **Quiet Reflection:** Spend quiet reflection, waiting on God and seeking His presence. Use this time to pray, meditate, and listen for His voice.
- **Breath Prayer:** Practice breath prayers, repeating a short prayer or Scripture verse as you breathe in and out. This can help you focus on God and find peace and renewal.
- **Physical Rest:** Ensure you get enough physical rest. Recognize that rest is a form of worship and a way to honor God's design for your body and spirit.

Prayer:

"Lord, thank You for Your promise to renew our strength when we wait on You. Help me to trust in Your power and timing and to find refreshment in Your presence. Renew my spirit and give me the strength to rise above challenges and continue my journey joyfully. In Jesus' name, Amen."

Sabbath Practice:

Dedicate part of your Sabbath to activities that bring spiritual refreshment and renewal.

- **Nature Walk:** Take a walk in nature, reflecting on God's creation and His promises. Use this time to pray and seek His presence.
- **Restful Activities:** Engage in activities that bring you peace and tranquility, such as reading a devotional, taking a nap, or enjoying a hobby that soothes your soul.

Reflect and Renew:

God promises to renew the strength of those who wait on Him. As you observe the Sabbath this week, rest in His presence and seek His spiritual refreshment. Trust in His power and timing, and let Him renew your strength for the journey ahead, knowing that He always provides for His children.

Week 31: Renewal in Prayer

Scripture Verse:

Matthew 6:6 (ESV) - "But when you pray, go into your room and shut the door and pray to your Father who is in secret. And your Father who sees in secret will reward you."

Reflection:

Matthew 6:6 emphasizes the importance of private, intimate prayer with God. Jesus encourages us to find a quiet place to pray, away from distractions and interruptions, where we can connect deeply with our Heavenly Father. This kind of prayer is personal and sincere, offering a space for spiritual refreshment and intimate communion with God.

Renewal in prayer involves setting aside time to be alone with God, pouring out our hearts, and listening for His guidance. The Sabbath provides a perfect opportunity to deepen our prayer life and find spiritual renewal. By dedicating time to private prayer, we open ourselves to God's presence and receive His peace and direction.

Practical Application:

This week, focus on renewing your spirit through private, intimate prayer with God.

- **Prayer Space:** Create a dedicated space for prayer in your home. This could be a quiet corner, a comfortable chair, or a room where you can be alone with God.
- **Prayer Schedule:** Set a regular time for private prayer each day. Use this time to talk to God, listen to His voice, and reflect on His Word.
- **Prayer Journal:** Keep a prayer journal to record your prayers, insights, and answers from God. This can help you track your spiritual growth and deepen your prayer life.

Prayer:

"Lord, thank You for the gift of prayer and the opportunity to connect with You personally and intimately. Help me find a quiet place to pray and dedicate time to seek Your presence. Renew my spirit through prayer and draw me closer to You. In Jesus' name, Amen."

Sabbath Practice:

Dedicate part of your Sabbath to deepening your prayer life and connecting with God personally.

- **Extended Prayer Time:** On the Sabbath, set aside an extended period for private prayer. Use this time to talk to God, listen to His voice, and reflect on His Word.
- **Prayer Walk:** Take a prayer walk, using the time to pray and meditate on Scripture. Let the act of walking help you focus and connect with God.

Reflect and Renew:

Private, intimate prayer is a powerful way to renew your spirit and connect with God. As you observe the Sabbath this week, dedicate time to deepening your prayer life and seeking God's presence. Let this prayer time bring peace, renewal, and a deeper connection with your Heavenly Father.

Week 32: Rest and Fasting

Scripture Verse:

Isaiah 58:6-12 (ESV) - "Is not this the fast that I choose: to loose the bonds of wickedness, to undo the straps of the yoke, to let the oppressed go free, and to break every yoke? Is it not to share your bread with the hungry and bring the homeless poor into your house when you see the naked, to cover him and not to hide yourself from your flesh? Then shall your light break forth like the dawn, and your healing shall spring up speedily; your righteousness shall go before you; the glory of the LORD shall be your rear guard. Then you shall call, and the LORD will answer; you shall cry, and he will say, 'Here I am.' If you take away the yoke from your midst, the pointing of the finger, and speaking wickedness, if you pour yourself out for the hungry and satisfy the desire of the afflicted, then shall your light rise in the darkness and your gloom be as the noonday. And the LORD will guide you continually, satisfy your desire in scorched places, and make your bones strong; and you shall be like a watered garden, like a spring of water, whose waters do not fail. And your ancient ruins shall be rebuilt; you shall raise the foundations of many generations; you shall be called the repairer of the breach, the restorer of streets to dwell in."

Reflection:

Isaiah 58:6-12 redefines fasting as more than just abstaining from food; it is a practice that involves justice, compassion, and generosity. According to God, true fasting is about losing the bonds of wickedness, sharing with the needy, and caring for the oppressed. This fasting brings spiritual renewal and healing, reflecting God's heart for justice and mercy.

Rest and fasting go hand in hand. Both involve setting aside physical desires to focus on spiritual growth and renewal. By incorporating practices of justice and compassion into our fasting, we align ourselves with God's purposes and experience deeper spiritual refreshment. The Sabbath provides an opportunity to reflect on these practices and to seek renewal through rest and fasting.

Practical Application:

This week, focus on the spiritual renewal of fasting and practicing justice and compassion.

- **Fasting Practice:** Choose a day to fast and abstain from food or a specific activity. Use the time to pray, reflect, and seek God's guidance.
- **Acts of Compassion:** Engage in acts of compassion and justice, such as feeding the hungry, helping people without homes, or supporting a charitable cause. Reflect on how these actions align with God's heart.
- **Reflection and Prayer:** Spend time reflecting on Isaiah 58:6-12, praying for God to reveal ways to practice true fasting.

Prayer:

"Lord, thank You for teaching us the true meaning of fasting. Please help me to practice justice and compassion and to seek spiritual renewal through rest and fasting. Guide me in aligning my actions with Your purposes, and may my life reflect Your heart for the needy and oppressed. In Jesus' name, Amen."

Sabbath Practice:

Incorporate fasting and acts of compassion into your Sabbath observance.

- **Fasting Reflection:** Spend part of your Sabbath reflecting on the purpose of fasting. Consider how you can incorporate fasting and compassionate actions into your spiritual practice.
- **Service Activity:** Plan a service activity that helps those in need, such as volunteering at a shelter, preparing meals for the hungry, or supporting a community project.

Reflect and Renew:

Fasting and rest are powerful practices for spiritual renewal. As you observe the Sabbath this week, reflect on how you can incorporate fasting and acts of compassion into your life. Seek spiritual refreshment through these practices, and align yourself with God's purposes of justice and mercy. Let this time of rest and fasting bring you closer to God and deepen your spiritual journey.

Summary of August: Spiritual Renewal through Rest

The theme for August is "Spiritual Renewal through Rest." This month, we have focused on how practices like immersing ourselves in God's Word, seeking spiritual refreshment, deepening our prayer life, and fasting can bring spiritual renewal. Each week, we explored how these practices can deepen our connection with God and refresh our souls.

Reflecting on the Month

As you reflect on the past month, consider how engaging in practices like immersing yourself in God's Word, seeking spiritual refreshment, deepening your prayer life, and fasting has impacted your spiritual life. How have these practices brought renewal and a deeper connection with God? Have you experienced a greater sense of peace, strength, and clarity?

- **Personal Reflections:** Spend time journaling about your experiences this month. What have you learned about spiritual renewal through rest? How have these insights transformed your approach to your spiritual practices and the Sabbath?
- **Gratitude:** Reflect on the moments when you felt the most renewed and connected to God through these practices. Write down these experiences and thank Him for His presence and guidance.

Invitation to Continue the Journey

The journey of spiritual renewal through rest is ongoing. As you move forward, carry the lessons and practices you have developed this month. Continue to seek opportunities to immerse yourself in God's Word, find spiritual refreshment, deepen your prayer life, and practice fasting.

- **Ongoing Practice:** Make the principles of immersing in Scripture, seeking spiritual refreshment, deepening prayer, and fasting a regular part of your Sabbath observance. Focus on how these practices can bring renewal and a deeper connection with God.
- **Community Sharing:** Share your insights and experiences with your faith community. Encourage others to embrace these practices and find spiritual renewal through rest.

May the foundation you have built this month continue to support and enrich your journey throughout the year. Embrace each day and each Sabbath with a renewed sense of peace, strength, and connection with God. Let His presence guide you into deeper spiritual renewal and fulfillment.

Looking Ahead

As you prepare to move into the next month of "The 7th Day" devotional, look forward to exploring new themes and insights about the Sabbath. Each month builds upon the previous one, offering a more profound understanding of rest and renewal.

In September, we will focus on "Embracing the Rhythm of Rest," exploring how trusting in God's provision, finding joy in the Sabbath, resting in His sovereignty, and recognizing the Sabbath as a sign of our covenant with God can deepen our spiritual lives. May you be blessed as you continue this journey, finding ever deeper peace and joy in the gift of the Sabbath.

September: Rest as Trust

Week 33: Trust in God's Provision

Scripture Verse:

Matthew 6:31-33 (ESV) - "Therefore do not be anxious, saying, 'What shall we eat?' or 'What shall we drink?' or 'What shall we wear?' For the Gentiles seek after all these things, and your heavenly Father knows that you need them all. But seek first the kingdom of God and his righteousness, and all these things will be added to you."

Reflection:

In Matthew 6:31-33, Jesus reassures us that God knows our needs and will provide for them. Instead of being consumed by worry, we are called to seek God's kingdom and righteousness first. This passage teaches us that trusting in God's provision allows us to rest in His care and focus on His purposes.

Trusting in God's provision frees us from the anxieties of daily life. The Sabbath is an opportunity to practice this trust by setting aside our worries and focusing on God's faithfulness. As we rest, we are reminded that God knows our needs and will provide for them in His perfect timing.

Practical Application:

This week, focus on trusting God's provision and letting go of anxieties about daily needs.

- **Daily Trust Exercise:** Each day, write down your worries and bring them to God in prayer, asking Him to help you trust in His provision.
- **Seek God's Kingdom:** Make seeking God's kingdom a priority daily. Reflect on how you can align your actions and decisions with His righteousness.
- **Sabbath Reflection:** Use your Sabbath to reflect on how God has provided for you in the past. Thank Him for His faithfulness and provision.

Prayer:

"Lord, thank You for knowing my needs and providing for me. Help me to trust in Your provision and to seek Your kingdom above all else. May I find peace and rest in Your care. In Jesus' name, Amen."

Sabbath Practice:

Dedicate your Sabbath to reflecting on God's provision and practicing trust.

- **Gratitude Walk:** Take a walk and use the time to thank God for His provision in your life. Reflect on specific ways He has cared for you.
- **Trust Journal:** Keep a journal where you write down instances of God's provision and care. Use this journal to remind yourself of His faithfulness.

Week 34: Trusting God's Plans

Scripture Verse:

Proverbs 3:5-6 (ESV) - "Trust in the LORD with all your heart, and do not lean on your understanding. In all your ways, acknowledge him, and he will direct your paths."

Reflection:

Proverbs 3:5-6 encourages us to trust the Lord with all our hearts and not rely on our understanding. Acknowledging God in all our ways means seeking His guidance and trusting His plans, even when we don't fully understand them. This kind of trust brings peace and direction to our lives.

Trusting in God's plans allows us to rest in His wisdom and timing. The Sabbath provides a special opportunity to surrender our plans to God and seek His guidance. As we rest, we are reminded that God's plans are perfect and that He will lead us on the right path.

Practical Application:

This week, focus on trusting in God's plans and seeking His guidance in all areas of your life.

- **Surrender Your Plans:** Pray each day that you will surrender your plans and decisions to God and ask for His guidance and wisdom.
- **Acknowledge God:** Make it a habit to acknowledge God in all your ways. Before making decisions, seek His direction and trust in His leadership.
- **Reflect on God's Guidance:** Use your Sabbath to reflect on how God has guided you in the past. Thank Him for His direction and wisdom.

Prayer:

"Lord, thank You for Your perfect plans and guiding me in all my ways. Help me to trust in You with all my heart and to acknowledge You in everything I do. May I find peace and direction as I rest in Your wisdom. In Jesus' name, Amen."

Sabbath Practice:

Dedicate part of your Sabbath to reflecting on God's plans and seeking His guidance.

- **Quiet Reflection:** Spend quiet reflection, asking God to reveal His plans for your life. Listen for His voice and direction.
- **Scripture Meditation:** Meditate on Proverbs 3:5-6, repeating the verses and allowing their truth to sink into your heart and mind.

Week 35: Leaning on God's Strength

Scripture Verse:

Isaiah 40:28-31 (ESV) - "Have you not known? Have you not heard? The LORD is the everlasting God, the Creator of the ends of the earth. He does not faint or grow weary; his understanding is unsearchable. He gives power to the faint and increases strength to him who has no might. Even youths shall faint and be weary, and young men shall fall exhausted, but they who wait for the LORD shall renew their strength; they shall mount up with wings like eagles; they shall run and not be weary; they shall walk and not faint."

Reflection:

Isaiah 40:28-31 reminds us of God's everlasting strength and power. Unlike us, God never grows weary or tired. When we feel weak and exhausted, we can lean on His strength and find renewal. Those who wait on the Lord will have their strength renewed and will be able to rise above their challenges.

Leaning on God's strength allows us to rest in His power and sufficiency. The Sabbath is an ideal time to seek God's strength and renewal. As we rest, we acknowledge our dependence on Him and allow His power to refresh us.

Practical Application:

This week, focus on leaning on God's strength and finding renewal in His power.

- **Daily Strength Prayer:** Pray for God's strength and renewal daily. Ask Him to refresh you and give you the energy to face your challenges.
- **Wait on the Lord:** Practice waiting on the Lord by setting aside time for quiet reflection and prayer. Use this time to seek His presence and strength.
- **Sabbath Renewal:** Use your Sabbath to rest and renew your strength. Engage in activities that refresh your body, mind, and spirit.

Prayer:

"Lord, thank You for Your everlasting strength and power. Help me to lean on You and to find renewal in Your presence. May I be refreshed and strengthened as I wait on You? In Jesus' name, Amen."

Sabbath Practice:

Dedicate part of your Sabbath to seeking God's strength and renewal.

- **Restful Activities:** Plan activities that help you rest and renew your strength, such as taking a nap, reading a devotional, or enjoying a nature walk.
- **Scripture Meditation:** Meditate on Isaiah 40:28-31, reflecting on God's strength and allowing His power to refresh you.

Reflect and Renew:

This week, as you lean on God's strength and embrace the renewal He offers, remember that His power is made perfect in your weakness. Waiting on the Lord is not a passive act but a deliberate choice to seek His presence and trust in His timing. Doing so allows His boundless energy and understanding to refresh and empower you. The Sabbath is a special time to practice this trust and renewal, but God's strength is available daily. Let His unending power uplift you, enabling you to face each challenge with renewed vigor and unwavering faith.

Week 36: Rest in God's Faithfulness

Scripture Verse:

Lamentations 3:22-24 (ESV) - "The steadfast love of the LORD never ceases; his mercies never come to an end; they are new every morning; great is your faithfulness. 'The LORD is my portion,' says my soul, 'therefore I will hope in him.'"

Reflection:

Lamentations 3:22-24 speaks of God's steadfast love and unending mercies. Every morning, we can experience His faithfulness anew. This passage reminds us that God is our portion and our hope. Resting in God's faithfulness allows us to find peace and assurance in His constant love and care.

Resting in God's faithfulness brings hope and renewal. The Sabbath provides a time to reflect on His mercies and to rest in His unchanging love. As we rest, we are reminded that God's faithfulness is great and that we can trust Him in all circumstances.

Practical Application:

This week, focus on resting in God's faithfulness and finding hope in His unending mercies.

- **Daily Gratitude:** Write down things you are thankful for daily, focusing on God's faithfulness and mercies. Use this practice to remind yourself of His constant care.
- **Hope in God:** Reflect on areas where you need to place your hope in God. Pray for His guidance and trust in His faithfulness.
- **Sabbath Reflection:** Use your Sabbath to reflect on God's steadfast love and mercies. Thank Him for His faithfulness, and find rest in His care.

Prayer:

"Lord, thank You for Your steadfast love and unending mercies. Help me to rest in Your faithfulness and to find hope in You. May Your constant care bring me peace and renewal. In Jesus' name, Amen."

Sabbath Practice:

Dedicate part of your Sabbath to reflecting on God's faithfulness and finding hope in His mercies.

- **Gratitude Journal:** Keep a journal of God's faithfulness. Write down instances where you have experienced His love and care.
- **Scripture Meditation:** Meditate on Lamentations 3:22-24, reflecting on God's steadfast love and allowing His faithfulness to bring you hope and peace.

Reflect and Renew:

Resting in God's faithfulness brings peace and hope. As you observe the Sabbath this week, reflect on His constant love and mercies. Let this reflection renew your spirit and deepen your trust in His unchanging faithfulness.

October: The Eternal Rest

Week 37: The Promise of Eternal Rest

Scripture Verse:

Hebrews 4:9-10 (ESV) - "So then, there remains a Sabbath rest for the people of God, for whoever has entered God's rest has also rested from his works as God did from his."

Reflection:

Hebrews 4:9-10 speaks of a Sabbath rest that remains for the people of God, pointing to an eternal rest that we will experience with God. As God rested from His works, we will rest from our labors and enter His perfect peace. This promise of eternal rest gives us hope and encouragement, knowing that our ultimate rest is found in God.

The Sabbath rest we observe each week is a foretaste of the eternal rest we will enjoy in God's presence. It reminds us that our work on earth is temporary and that we can look forward to a time when we will fully rest in God's completed work.

Practical Application:

This week, focus on the promise of eternal rest and how it impacts your perspective on work and rest.

- **Reflect on Eternity:** Reflect each day on the promise of eternal rest. Consider how this promise affects your attitude toward work and rest in this life.
- **Sabbath Anticipation:** Use your Sabbath to anticipate the eternal rest that awaits you. Rest in the knowledge that God has prepared a place of perfect peace for you.
- **Encourage Others:** Share the hope of eternal rest with others. Encourage them to find peace and assurance in the promise of God's eternal Sabbath rest.

Prayer:

"Lord, thank You for the promise of eternal rest. Help me to live with the hope and assurance that my ultimate rest is found in You. May this promise give me peace and perspective as I navigate the challenges of this life? In Jesus' name, Amen."

Sabbath Practice:

Dedicate part of your Sabbath to reflecting on the promise of eternal rest.

- **Quiet Reflection:** Spend quiet reflection, meditating on Hebrews 4:9-10 and the promise of eternal rest. Allow this truth to bring you peace and assurance.
- **Worship and Praise:** Include worship and praise in your Sabbath observance, focusing on God's promise of eternal rest and the hope it brings.

Reflect and Renew:

Let the eternal rest promise you hope and assurance as you rest this week. Our earthly struggles and labors are temporary, but God has prepared an everlasting Sabbath for us in His presence. Embrace the peace from knowing your ultimate rest is secure in Him. Let this promise shape your perspective, bringing comfort and encouragement as you look forward to the day you fully enter God's perfect rest.

Week 38: The Hope of Heaven

Scripture Verse:

Revelation 14:13 (ESV) - "And I heard a voice from heaven saying, 'Write this: Blessed are the dead who die in the Lord from now on.' 'Blessed indeed,' says the Spirit, 'that they may rest from their labors, for their deeds follow them!'"

Reflection:

Revelation 14:13 speaks of the blessed rest that awaits those who die in the Lord. This verse promises that we will rest from our labors and be rewarded for our faithful service in heaven. The hope of heaven gives us strength and encouragement to persevere in our faith and work.

The hope of heaven assures us that our efforts and struggles in this life are not in vain. Knowing that we will rest in God's presence and receive His reward motivates us to live faithfully and to serve Him with all our hearts.

Practical Application:

This week, focus on the hope of heaven and how it influences your life and work.

- **Heavenly Perspective:** Reflect on the hope of heaven and how it affects your daily life. Consider how the promise of eternal rest motivates you to live faithfully and serve God.
- **Encourage Others:** Share the hope of heaven with others who may be struggling or discouraged. Remind them of the blessed rest that awaits those who die in the Lord.
- **Faithful Service:** Evaluate how you can serve God more faithfully in your life and work. Let the hope of heaven inspire you to persevere and remain steadfast.

Prayer:

"Lord, thank You for the hope of heaven and the promise of eternal rest. Help me to live with this hope and to serve You faithfully. May the assurance of heavenly rest give me strength and encouragement daily. In Jesus' name, Amen."

Sabbath Practice:

Dedicate part of your Sabbath to reflecting on the hope of heaven and the rest that awaits you.

- **Meditative Prayer:** Spend time in contemplative prayer, focusing on Revelation 14:13 and the hope of heaven. Allow this promise to comfort and motivate you.
- **Worship and Reflection:** Include worship and reflection in your Sabbath observance, praising God for the hope of heaven and the blessed rest that awaits you.

Reflect and Renew:

As you rest this week, let the hope of heaven fill you with strength and encouragement. The promise of eternal rest in God's presence assures you that your labors are not in vain and that a glorious reward awaits. Embrace this hope and let it inspire you to live faithfully and serve God with all your heart. Allow the assurance of heavenly rest to comfort you in times of struggle and motivate you to persevere in your faith journey.

Week 39: Rest in God's Kingdom

Scripture Verse:

Matthew 25:34 (ESV) - "Then the King will say to those on his right, 'Come, you whom my Father blesses, inherit the kingdom prepared for you from the foundation of the world.'"

Reflection:

Matthew 25:34 highlights the invitation to inherit God's kingdom, which has been prepared for us from the foundation of the world. This verse reminds us that we are blessed by the Father and called to enter into His eternal kingdom. The rest we experience in God's kingdom is a culmination of His promises and blessings.

Resting in God's kingdom means experiencing His peace, joy, and presence. It is a place of eternal rest where we are free from the burdens and struggles of this world. This promise of rest in God's kingdom gives us hope and encourages us to live as faithful servants of the King.

Practical Application:

This week, focus on the promise of rest in God's kingdom and how it shapes your life and faith.

- **Kingdom Perspective:** Reflect on the promise of inheriting God's kingdom and consider how this promise influences your daily decisions and actions.
- **Faithful Living:** Strive to live as a faithful servant of God's kingdom. Let the promise of rest in His kingdom motivate you to serve Him with joy and dedication.
- **Encourage Others:** Share the promise of God's kingdom with others, encouraging them to live faithfully and look forward to the eternal rest that awaits.

Prayer:

"Lord, thank You for the promise of rest in Your kingdom. Please help me to live as a faithful servant. I am looking forward to the inheritance You have prepared for me. May this promise give me hope and strength in my daily life? In Jesus' name, Amen."

Sabbath Practice:

Dedicate part of your Sabbath to reflecting on the promise of rest in God's kingdom.

- **Quiet Meditation:** Spend quiet meditation, focusing on Matthew 25:34 and the promise of inheriting God's kingdom. Allow this promise to fill you with hope and joy.
- **Worship and Praise:** Include worship and praise in your Sabbath observance, celebrating the promise of rest in God's kingdom and His eternal blessings.

Reflect and Renew:

As you rest this week, let the promise of inheriting God's kingdom fill you with hope and joy. The eternal rest that awaits you in God's presence is a culmination of His love and faithfulness. Embrace this promise and let it inspire you to live faithfully as a servant of the King.

Every act of service, every moment of faithfulness, brings you closer to the eternal rest and joy of God's kingdom. Let the vision of your inheritance in God's kingdom sustain you in times of struggle and challenge. Remember that you are blessed by the Father, and the kingdom prepared for you is a place of peace, joy, and eternal rest. Let this promise guide your actions, fill your heart with hope, and encourage you to persevere in your faith journey.

Week 40: Eternal Sabbath

Scripture Verse:

Revelation 21:3-4 (ESV) - "And I heard a loud voice from the throne saying, 'Behold, the dwelling place of God is with man. He will dwell with them; they will be his people, and God himself will be with them as their God. He will wipe away every tear from their eyes, and death shall be no more, neither shall there be mourning, nor crying, nor pain anymore, for the former things have passed away.'"

Reflection:

Revelation 21:3-4 describes the ultimate fulfillment of God's promise of an eternal Sabbath. In this new creation, God will dwell with His people, and all suffering, pain, and death will be eradicated. This eternal Sabbath represents the culmination of God's redemptive plan, where we will experience perfect peace and rest in His presence forever.

The eternal Sabbath is the hope and joy of every believer. It is when all things will be made new, and we will live in perfect harmony with God. This vision of the future gives us hope and perseverance as we navigate the trials and challenges of this life.

Practical Application:

This week, focus on the promise of the eternal Sabbath and how it impacts your life and faith.

- **Eternal Perspective:** Reflect on the vision of the eternal Sabbath described in Revelation 21:3-4. Consider how this vision shapes your hope and perseverance in daily life.
- **Encourage Others:** Share the promise of the eternal Sabbath with others, offering hope and encouragement to those suffering or struggling.
- **Live in Hope:** Let the promise of the eternal Sabbath inspire you to live with hope and joy, knowing that God's ultimate plan is for your perfect rest and peace.

Prayer:

"Lord, thank You for the promise of the eternal Sabbath, where we will dwell with You and experience perfect peace and rest. Help me live with this hope and persevere through this life's challenges. May Your vision of the eternal Sabbath bring me joy and strength. In Jesus' name, Amen."

Sabbath Practice:

Dedicate part of your Sabbath to reflecting on the promise of the eternal Sabbath and finding hope in God's ultimate plan.

- **Vision Meditation:** Spend time meditating on Revelation 21:3-4, envisioning the eternal Sabbath and the perfect rest it promises. Let this vision fill you with hope and anticipation.
- **Worship and Celebration:** Include worship and celebration in your Sabbath observance, praising God for the promise of the eternal Sabbath and the joy of His presence.

Reflect and Renew:

As you rest this week, let the vision of the eternal Sabbath bring you hope and joy. The promise of dwelling with God, free from all pain and suffering, is a powerful source of encouragement. This eternal perspective can transform how you face the difficulties and trials of this life.

Remember that every tear will be wiped away, and all sorrow will be turned to joy in God's perfect presence. This hope allows you to live with joy and purpose, knowing that the ultimate rest and peace are guaranteed. Embrace this promise, let it guide your actions, and find comfort in the assurance that God's perfect Sabbath awaits you. As you anticipate this eternal rest, allow it to deepen your faith and strengthen your resolve to live fully for Him, confident in His everlasting love and grace.

Summary of October: The Eternal Rest

The theme for October is "The Eternal Rest." Throughout this month, we have focused on the promises of eternal rest, the hope of heaven, resting in God's kingdom, and the vision of the eternal Sabbath. Each week, we explored different aspects of how these promises provide hope, encouragement, and strength as we navigate our earthly journey.

Reflecting on the Month

As you reflect on the past month, consider how the promises of eternal rest have impacted your life. How has focusing on the hope of heaven, the promise of inheriting God's kingdom, and the vision of the eternal Sabbath deepened your faith and provided you with encouragement and strength? Have you experienced greater peace and hope as you navigate your earthly journey?

- **Personal Reflections:** Spend time journaling about your experiences this month. What have you learned about the promises of eternal rest, and how have they transformed your approach to your daily life and faith?
- **Gratitude:** Reflect on the moments when you felt the most connected to God through the hope of eternal rest. Write down these experiences and thank Him for His promises and faithfulness.

Invitation to Continue the Journey

The journey of embracing the promises of eternal rest is ongoing. As you move forward, carry the lessons and insights you have developed this month. Continue to seek opportunities to reflect on these promises, finding hope and encouragement in God's eternal plan.

- **Ongoing Practice:** Make the principles of hope, faith, and perseverance a regular part of your Sabbath observance. Keep focusing on how the promises of eternal rest can bring peace and joy to your life.
- **Community Sharing:** Share your insights and experiences with your faith community. Encourage others to embrace the hope of eternal rest and to find strength in God's promises.

May the foundation you have built this month continue to support and enrich your journey throughout the year. Embrace each Sabbath with renewed hope, joy, and connection with God. Let His promises of eternal rest guide you into deeper faith and perseverance.

Looking Ahead

As you prepare to move into the next month of "The 7th Day" devotional, look forward to exploring new themes and insights about the Sabbath. Each month builds upon the previous one, offering a more profound understanding of rest and renewal.

In November, we will focus on "Gratitude and Reflection," exploring how practicing gratitude and reflecting on God's goodness can deepen our Sabbath experience and enrich our spiritual lives. May you be blessed as you continue this journey, finding ever deeper peace and joy in the gift of the Sabbath.

November: Community and Rest

Week 41: Sabbath in Community

Scripture Verse:

Acts 2:42-47 (ESV) - "And they devoted themselves to the apostles' teaching and the fellowship, the breaking of bread and the prayers. And awe came upon every soul, and many wonders and signs were done through the apostles. And all who believed were together and had all things in common. They sold their possessions and belongings and distributed the proceeds as needed. And day by day, attending the temple together and breaking bread in their homes, they received their food with glad and generous hearts, praising God and having favor with all the people. And the Lord added to their number day by day those who were being saved."

Reflection:

Acts 2:42-47 paints a beautiful picture of the early Christian community. They devoted themselves to teaching, fellowship, breaking bread, and prayer. This passage highlights the importance of community in the life of believers. They shared their resources, supported one another, and experienced the power of God together.

The Sabbath provides a special opportunity to experience community. Gathering with fellow believers to worship, share meals, and support one another enhances our spiritual journey. It allows us to grow together, bear each other's burdens, and celebrate God's goodness collectively.

Practical Application:

This week, focus on experiencing the Sabbath in the community and strengthening your relationships with fellow believers.

- **Fellowship Time:** Dedicate time to fellowship with other believers. Invite friends or family for a meal, attend a church gathering, or participate in a small group.
- **Shared Worship:** Engage in shared worship experiences. Attend a church service, join a prayer group, or participate in communal Bible study.
- **Acts of Service:** Find opportunities to serve others in your community. Share your resources, offer help, and support those in need.

Prayer:

"Lord, thank You for the gift of community and the opportunity to experience the Sabbath with others. Help me to grow in fellowship, to support and be supported by fellow believers, and to experience Your presence in our midst. In Jesus' name, Amen."

Sabbath Practice:

Dedicate part of your Sabbath to community activities and fellowship.

- **Communal Meal:** Plan a meal with friends or family. Use this time to share, connect, and celebrate God's blessings together.
- **Group Worship:** Participate in a group worship activity. Attend a church service or join a prayer meeting to

worship God with others.

Reflect and Renew:

As you rest this week, embrace the gift of community. Sharing the Sabbath with others brings richness and depth to your spiritual journey. Let the fellowship of believers encourage and strengthen you and find joy in worshipping and serving together.

Week 42: Encouraging One Another

Scripture Verse:

Hebrews 10:24-25 (ESV) - "And let us consider how to stir up one another to love and good works, not neglecting to meet together, as is the habit of some, but encouraging one another, and all the more as you see the Day drawing near."

Reflection:

Hebrews 10:24-25 emphasizes the importance of meeting together and encouraging one another. We believers are called to spur each other towards love and good works. Regular fellowship and mutual encouragement are vital for our spiritual growth and perseverance.

The Sabbath is a perfect time to practice encouragement within the community. Gathering with others, we can offer support, share burdens, and motivate one another to live out our faith. Encouragement strengthens our bonds and helps us remain steadfast in our journey.

Practical Application:

This week, focus on encouraging others and fostering a spirit of mutual support.

- **Encouragement Notes:** Write notes of encouragement to friends, family, or fellow church members. Let them know you are praying for them and appreciate their faith.
- **Positive Conversations:** Engage in conversations that uplift and inspire. Share positive stories, affirm others, and speak words of encouragement.
- **Group Activities:** Plan group activities that promote love and good work. This could include volunteering together, organizing a community project, or supporting a charitable cause.

Prayer:

"Lord, thank You for the gift of encouragement and the power of community. Please help me to be a source of support and motivation for others. May we spur one another on to love, do good works, and find strength in our fellowship. In Jesus' name, Amen."

Sabbath Practice:

Dedicate part of your Sabbath to encouraging others and building a supportive community.

- **Encouragement Circle:** Gather a group of friends or family and take turns sharing words of encouragement and appreciation for one another.
- **Prayer Partners:** Pair up with a prayer partner to pray for each other's needs and offer support throughout the week.

Reflect and Renew:

As you rest this week, focus on the power of encouragement. Lifting one another in love and good works strengthens our faith and deepens our community bonds. Let your words and actions be a source of inspiration and support, reflecting the love of Christ to those around you.

Week 43: Bearing Each Other's Burdens

Scripture Verse:
Galatians 6:2 (ESV) - "Bear one another's burdens, and so fulfill the law of Christ."

Reflection:
Galatians 6:2 calls us to bear one another's burdens, fulfilling the law of Christ through acts of love and support. This verse emphasizes the importance of compassion and empathy within the Christian community. By helping each other, we reflect Christ's love and build a stronger, more supportive community.

The Sabbath is an opportunity to practice bearing each other's burdens. By coming together, we can share our struggles, offer support, and find comfort in the presence of fellow believers. This mutual care strengthens our relationships and helps us to grow in faith and love.

Practical Application:
This week, focus on bearing the burdens of others and offering compassionate support.

- **Active Listening:** Listen to others' struggles and concerns. Offer a listening ear and an empathetic heart, showing genuine care.
- **Practical Help:** Provide practical help to those in need. This could include running errands, offering a ride, or helping with household tasks.
- **Prayer Support:** Pray for those who are burdened. Lift their needs to God and ask for His comfort and provision.

Prayer:
"Lord, thank You for the call to bear one another's burdens. Help me to be compassionate and supportive, reflecting Your love for those around me. May our community be strengthened as we care for each other in Your name. In Jesus' name, Amen."

Sabbath Practice:
Dedicate part of your Sabbath to bearing the burdens of others and practicing compassionate support.

- **Supportive Gathering:** Host a gathering where people can share their burdens and pray for one another. Create a safe space for open and honest sharing.
- **Service Project:** Organize a service project to help those in need. This could be within your church community or the wider community.

Reflect and Renew:
As you rest this week, focus on the call to bear one another's burdens. Offering compassionate support strengthens our community and fulfills the law of Christ. Let your actions reflect His love, and find joy in helping others carry their burdens.

Week 44: Fellowship and Rest

Scripture Verse:
1 Thessalonians 5:11 (ESV) - "Therefore encourage one another and build one another up, just as you are doing."

Reflection:
1 Thessalonians 5:11 encourages us to build one another up through mutual encouragement and support. Fellowship and rest are intertwined, as spending time with fellow believers refreshes our spirits and strengthens our faith. Building each other creates a supportive and loving community where everyone can thrive.

The Sabbath is a time to rest, rejuvenate, and engage in meaningful fellowship. By encouraging one another, we strengthen our bonds and find renewed energy and joy in our faith journey.

Practical Application:

This week, focus on fostering fellowship and rest through encouragement and support.

- **Fellowship Activities:** Plan activities that promote fellowship and rest, such as a shared meal, a nature walk, or a game night.
- **Encouragement Notes:** Continue writing notes of encouragement, highlighting the positive qualities and contributions of others.
- **Restful Gatherings:** Create spaces for restful gathering spaces where people can relax, share, and enjoy each other's company without pressure or stress.

Prayer:

"Lord, thank You for the gift of fellowship and the opportunity to build one another up. Please help us to encourage and support each other, finding rest and joy in our shared faith. May our community be a source of strength and renewal. In Jesus' name, Amen."

Sabbath Practice:

Dedicate part of your Sabbath to fellowship and rest, focusing on encouraging and building each other up.

- **Shared Meal:** Host or participate in a meal with friends or family. Use this time to connect, relax, and enjoy each other's company.
- **Reflection and Prayer:** Reflect on the week and pray for your community. Ask God to strengthen your bonds and to help you build each other up.

Reflect and Renew:

As you rest this week, embrace the power of fellowship and encouragement. Building one another up creates a strong, supportive community that reflects the love of Christ. Find joy and renewal in your shared faith, and let your fellowship be a source of strength and rest for all.

Summary of November: Community and Rest

Throughout November, we have focused on the importance of community and rest, exploring how fellowship, encouragement, and mutual support can deepen our faith and provide renewal. Each week, we have delved into different aspects of building a strong, supportive Christian community.

Reflecting on the Month

Reflecting on the past month, consider how focusing on community and rest has impacted your life. How has engaging in fellowship, encouragement, and mutual support deepened your faith and provided renewal? Have you experienced a greater sense of connection and strength within your community?

- **Personal Reflections:** Spend time journaling about your experiences this month. What have you learned about the importance of community and rest, and how has it transformed your approach to the Sabbath and daily life?
- **Gratitude:** Reflect on the moments when you felt most connected to others and supported in your faith journey. Write down these experiences and thank God for the gift of community.

Invitation to Continue the Journey

The journey of building a strong, supportive community is ongoing. As you move forward, carry the lessons and practices you have developed this month. Continue to seek opportunities to foster fellowship, offer encouragement, and support one another.

- **Ongoing Practice:** Make fellowship, encouragement, and mutual support a regular part of your Sabbath observance. Keep focusing on how these practices can strengthen your community and provide renewal.
- **Community Sharing:** Share your insights and experiences with your faith community. Encourage others to embrace the importance of community and rest.

May the foundation you have built this month continue to support and enrich your journey throughout the year. Embrace each Sabbath with a renewed sense of connection, joy, and support within your community. Let your fellowship and mutual encouragement guide you into deeper faith and renewal.

LOOKING AHEAD

As you prepare to move into the next month of "The 7th Day" devotional, look forward to exploring new themes and insights about the Sabbath. Each month builds upon the previous one, offering a more profound understanding of rest and renewal.

In December, we will focus on "Advent and Anticipation," exploring how the season of Advent prepares our hearts for the coming of Christ and how anticipation can deepen our spiritual journey. May you be blessed as you continue this journey, finding ever deeper peace and joy in the gift of the Sabbath.

December: Celebrating Rest

Week 45: The Joy of Rest

Scripture Verse:

Zephaniah 3:17 (ESV) - "The LORD your God is in your midst, a mighty one who will save; he will rejoice over you with gladness; he will quiet you by his love; he will exult over you with loud singing."

Reflection:

Zephaniah 3:17 speaks of the Lord's presence and joy over His people. God's love brings quietness and rest, and He rejoices over us with gladness. This verse reminds us of the deep joy of resting in God's love and presence.

Celebrating rest involves recognizing the joy that God takes in us and allowing His love to quiet our hearts. Resting in His presence brings us peace and joy, knowing God delights in us and saves us.

Practical Application:

This week, focus on finding joy in rest by experiencing God's love and presence.

- **Quiet Time:** Set aside time each day for quiet reflection, allowing God's love to bring you peace and joy.
- **Worship Music:** Listen to worship songs that celebrate God's love and joy. Let the music quiet your heart and fill you with His presence.
- **Joyful Activities:** Engage in activities that bring you joy and help you rest in God's love, such as spending time in nature, reading a good book, or enjoying a hobby.

Prayer:

"Lord, thank You for the joy of rest and your love for me. Help me to quiet my heart in Your presence and to find deep joy in resting in Your love. May Your joy fill me and bring me peace. In Jesus' name, Amen."

Sabbath Practice:

Dedicate part of your Sabbath to celebrating the joy of rest.

- **Joyful Reflection:** Spend time reflecting on Zephaniah 3:17, allowing the verse to remind you of God's love and joy over you.
- **Worship and Praise:** Include joyful worship and praise in your Sabbath observance, celebrating the joy of rest in God's presence.

Reflect and Renew:

As you rest this week, embrace the joy of God's love. Let His presence quiet your heart and fill you with gladness. Celebrate the joy of rest, knowing that God delights in you and rejoices over you with singing.

Week 46: Celebrating God's Goodness

Scripture Verse:

Psalm 92:1-4 (ESV) - "It is good to give thanks to the LORD, to sing praises to your name, O Most High; to declare your steadfast love in the morning, and your faithfulness by night, to the music of the lute and the harp, to the melody of the lyre. For you, O LORD, have made me glad by your work; at the works of your hands, I sing for joy."

Reflection:

Psalm 92:1-4 emphasizes the goodness of giving thanks and singing praises to the Lord. Celebrating God's goodness involves acknowledging His steadfast love and faithfulness. The psalmist finds joy in God's works and praises Him for His mighty deeds.

Celebrating God's goodness on the Sabbath allows us to reflect on His love and faithfulness. It's a time to sing praises, give thanks, and find joy in the works of His hands. Recognizing God's goodness brings gladness to our hearts and deepens our appreciation for His blessings.

Practical Application:

This week, focus on celebrating God's goodness through praise and thanksgiving.

- **Morning and Evening Praise:** Start and end your day by declaring God's steadfast love and faithfulness. Make it a habit to praise Him in the morning and evening.
- **Musical Worship:** Incorporate music into your worship. Sing praises, play an instrument, or listen to worship music that celebrates God's goodness.
- **Thanksgiving Journal:** Keep a journal of God's works. Write down moments when you have experienced His goodness and faithfulness.

Prayer:

"Lord, thank You for Your steadfast love and faithfulness. Help me celebrate Your goodness and sing praises in Your name. May my heart be filled with joy as I reflect on the works of Your hands. In Jesus' name, Amen."

Sabbath Practice:

Dedicate part of your Sabbath to celebrating God's goodness through praise and thanksgiving.

- **Praise Walk:** Walk in nature, praising God for His creation and goodness. Use this time to reflect on His works and to give thanks.
- **Musical Worship:** Spend time in musical worship, singing praises and playing instruments to celebrate God's goodness.

Reflect and Renew:

As you rest this week, celebrate God's goodness. Let your heart be filled with joy as you praise His steadfast love and faithfulness. Recognize His mighty works and find gladness in His presence.

Week 47: Rest in Thanksgiving

Scripture Verse:

1 Thessalonians 5:16-18 (ESV) - "Rejoice always, pray without ceasing, give thanks in all circumstances; for this is the will of God in Christ Jesus for you."

Reflection:

1 Thessalonians 5:16-18 encourages us always to rejoice, pray, and give thanks in all circumstances. Thanksgiving is a powerful practice that shifts our focus from our challenges to God's blessings. Resting in thanksgiving involves cultivating a heart of gratitude and recognizing God's goodness in every situation.

Giving thanks in all circumstances lets us find peace and rest, knowing God is at work. It reminds us to remain joyful, prayerful, and thankful, trusting that God's will is for our good.

Practical Application:

This week, focus on resting in thanksgiving and cultivating a heart of gratitude.

- **Daily Gratitude:** Write down things you are thankful for each day. Reflect on God's blessings and express your gratitude in prayer.
- **Joyful Prayer:** Practice praying with joy and thanksgiving. Include moments of praise and thanksgiving in your prayers, regardless of your circumstances.
- **Thankful Conversations:** Engage in conversations that focus on gratitude. Please share what you are grateful for with others and encourage them to do the same.

Prayer:

"Lord, thank You for Your goodness and blessings. Help me to cultivate a heart of gratitude and to give thanks in all circumstances. May my Thanksgiving bring me peace and rest in Your presence. In Jesus' name, Amen."

Sabbath Practice:

Dedicate part of your Sabbath to resting in thanksgiving and expressing gratitude.

- **Gratitude Walk:** Take a gratitude walk and reflect on what you are thankful for. Use this time to thank God for His blessings.
- **Thanksgiving Journal:** Write in your Thanksgiving journal, reflecting on God's goodness and expressing gratitude.

Reflect and Renew:

As you rest this week, embrace the power of thanksgiving. Let a heart of gratitude bring you peace and rest, knowing God is at work in every circumstance. Celebrate His goodness and find joy in giving thanks.

Week 48: Reflecting on God's Gifts

Scripture Verse:

James 1:17 (ESV) - "Every good gift and every perfect gift is from above, coming down from the Father of lights, with whom there is no variation or shadow due to change."

Reflection:

James 1:17 reminds us that every good and perfect gift comes from God. Reflecting on God's gifts allows us to see His hand at work in our lives and to recognize His unchanging goodness. It encourages us to appreciate our received blessings and thank God for His provision.

Reflecting on God's gifts helps us cultivate a grateful heart and acknowledge His constant presence and faithfulness. Focusing on His gifts, we deepen our relationship and find joy in His blessings.

Practical Application:

This week, focus on reflecting on God's gifts and appreciating His blessings.

- **Gift Reflection:** Spend time each day reflecting on the good and perfect gifts you have received from God. Acknowledge His provision and give thanks.
- **Blessings Journal:** Keep a journal of the blessings you receive. Write down how God has provided for you and how His gifts have impacted your life.
- **Sharing Blessings:** Share the story of God's gifts in your life with others. Encourage them by testifying to His goodness and faithfulness.

Prayer:

"Lord, thank You for every good and perfect gift You have given me. Help me recognize Your hand at work and appreciate Your blessings. May I always give thanks and celebrate Your unchanging goodness. In Jesus' name, Amen."

Sabbath Practice:

Dedicate part of your Sabbath to reflecting on God's gifts and expressing gratitude for His blessings.

- **Quiet Reflection:** Spend quiet reflection, focusing on James 1:17 and the gifts you have received from God. Let this time deepen your appreciation for His goodness.
- **Sharing Blessings:** Reflect on God's gifts with friends or family and use this time to celebrate His blessings together.

Reflect and Renew:

As you rest this week, take time to reflect on God's good and perfect gifts. Let your heart be filled with gratitude as you recognize His provision and celebrate His unchanging goodness. Find joy in His blessings, and let this reflection deepen your relationship with Him.

Summary of December: Celebrating Rest

Throughout December, we have focused on celebrating rest, exploring how joy, thanksgiving, and reflection on God's gifts enrich our spiritual journey. Each week, we have delved into finding joy in rest, celebrating God's goodness, resting in thanksgiving, and reflecting on God's gifts.

Reflecting on the Month

Reflecting on the past month, consider how celebrating rest has impacted your life. How has focusing on joy, thanksgiving, and reflection deepened your faith and provided renewal? Have you experienced greater peace and gratitude as you celebrated God's goodness and gifts?

- **Personal Reflections:** Spend time journaling about your experiences this month. What have you learned about celebrating rest, and how has it transformed your approach to the Sabbath and daily life?
- **Gratitude:** Reflect on the moments when you felt most connected to God through joy, thanksgiving, and reflection. Write down these experiences and thank Him for His blessings and faithfulness.

Invitation to Continue the Journey

The journey of celebrating rest and embracing God's gifts is ongoing. As you move forward, carry the lessons and practices you have developed this month. Continue to seek opportunities to celebrate joy, express gratitude, and reflect on God's blessings.

- **Ongoing Practice:** Make joy, thanksgiving, and reflection a regular part of your Sabbath observance. Keep focusing on how these practices can deepen your faith and provide renewal.
- **Community Sharing:** Share your insights and experiences with your faith community. Encourage others to embrace the joy of rest and to celebrate God's goodness and gifts.

May the foundation you have built this month continue to support and enrich your journey throughout the year. Embrace each Sabbath with a renewed sense of joy, gratitude, and reflection on God's goodness. Let His blessings guide you into deeper faith and renewal.

Looking Ahead

As you prepare to move into the next year of "The 7th Day" devotional, look forward to exploring new themes and insights about the Sabbath. Each month builds upon the previous one, offering a more profound understanding of rest and renewal.

May you be blessed as you continue this journey, finding ever deeper peace and joy in the gift of the Sabbath.

5th Sunday Reflections

These 5th Sunday reflections provide deeper insights and overarching themes that complement the regular weekly reflections. Use these reflections on months with five Sundays to enrich your spiritual journey and enhance your Sabbath observance.

5th Sunday Reflection 1: The Gift of Silence

Scripture Verse:

Psalm 46:10 (ESV) - "Be still, and know that I am God. I will be exalted among the nations. I will be exalted in the earth!"

Reflection:

In our busy lives, the gift of silence allows us to hear God's voice more clearly. Psalm 46:10 calls us to be still and recognize God's sovereignty. Silence helps us to quiet our minds and focus on His presence, deepening our relationship with Him.

Practical Application:

- **Silent Retreat:** Dedicate a portion of your Sabbath to a silent retreat. Spend time in quiet reflection and listen to God's voice.
- **Mindful Silence:** Practice moments of silence throughout your week. Use these times to pray and focus on God's presence.

Prayer:

"Lord, help me to embrace the gift of silence and to be still in Your presence. May I hear Your voice and deepen my relationship with You through quiet reflection. In Jesus' name, Amen."

Sabbath Practice:

- **Silent Walk:** Take a walk in silence, focusing on the sounds of nature and God's creation. Use this time to meditate on His presence.

Reflect and Renew:

Embrace the gift of silence to deepen your connection with God. Let moments of stillness refresh your spirit and bring clarity to your mind.

5th Sunday Reflection 2: The Power of Forgiveness

Scripture Verse:

Ephesians 4:32 (ESV) - "Be kind to one another, tenderhearted, forgiving one another, as God in Christ forgave you."

Reflection:

Forgiveness is a powerful act that brings healing and restoration. Ephesians 4:32 reminds us to forgive others as God has forgiven us in Christ. Practicing forgiveness frees us from bitterness and allows us to experience God's peace.

Practical Application:

- **Forgiveness Prayer:** Spend prayer, asking God to help you forgive those who wronged you.
- **Reconciliation:** Reach out to someone you must forgive or seek forgiveness from. Take steps toward reconciliation and healing.

Prayer:

"Lord, thank You for the gift of forgiveness. Help me to forgive others as You have forgiven me. May Your peace fill my heart as I let go of bitterness and embrace Your love. In Jesus' name, Amen."

Sabbath Practice:

- **Forgiveness Reflection:** Dedicate part of your Sabbath to reflecting on areas where you need to offer or seek forgiveness. Write a letter or journal about your thoughts and feelings.

Reflect and Renew:

Forgiveness brings freedom and peace. Embrace the power of forgiveness and allow God's grace to heal your heart and restore your relationships.

5th Sunday Reflection 3: The Beauty of Creation

Scripture Verse:

Psalm 19:1 (ESV) - "The heavens declare the glory of God, and the sky above proclaims his handiwork."

Reflection:

Psalm 19:1 celebrates the beauty and majesty of God's creation. Observing the natural world reminds us of God's creativity and power. The Sabbath is a perfect time to appreciate and connect with God's creation, finding rest and inspiration in its beauty.

Practical Application:

- **Nature Walk:** Spend time outdoors observing and appreciating nature's beauty. Reflect on how creation reveals God's glory.
- **Creation Care:** Commit to caring for the environment. Consider ways to reduce your ecological footprint and protect God's creation.

Prayer:

"Lord, thank You for the beauty of creation. Help me to see Your glory in the world around me and to care for the earth as a steward of Your handiwork. In Jesus' name, Amen."

Sabbath Practice:

- **Outdoor Worship:** Spend part of your Sabbath in an outdoor setting. Worship God through song, prayer, or quiet reflection surrounded by His creation.

Reflect and Renew:

The beauty of creation reflects God's glory. Let the natural world inspire you to worship and remind you of His greatness and creativity.

5th Sunday Reflection 4: The Joy of Generosity

Scripture Verse:

2 Corinthians 9:7 (ESV) - "Each one must give as he has decided in his heart, not reluctantly or under compulsion, for God loves a cheerful giver."

Reflection:

Generosity expresses God's love and provision. 2 Corinthians 9:7 encourages us to give cheerfully and willingly. Practicing generosity brings joy to both the giver and the receiver, reflecting God's abundant grace.

Practical Application:

- **Acts of Kindness:** Look for opportunities to practice generosity through acts of kindness. Help a neighbor,

support a charitable cause, or share your resources with those in need.
- **Generosity Journal:** Keep a journal of your experiences with generosity. Reflect on how giving impacts your heart and the lives of others.

Prayer:
"Lord, thank You for the joy of generosity. Help me to give cheerfully and willingly, reflecting Your love and grace. May my generosity bring joy and blessing to others. In Jesus' name, Amen."

Sabbath Practice:
- **Generosity Reflection:** Consider ways to be generous with your time, talents, and resources. Then, make a plan to put these ideas into action.

Reflect and Renew:
Generosity brings joy and reflects God's love. Embrace the joy of giving and let your acts of kindness make a difference in the lives of others.

5th Sunday Reflection 5: Trusting God's Timing

Scripture Verse:
Ecclesiastes 3:1 (ESV) - "For everything, there is a season and a time for every matter under heaven."

Reflection:
Ecclesiastes 3:1 reminds us that God has a perfect timing for everything. Trusting His timing means surrendering our plans and embracing His divine schedule. The Sabbath is a time to rest in God's timing and to trust that He is in control.

Practical Application:

- **Surrender Prayer:** Spend prayer, surrendering your plans and timelines to God. Ask for patience and trust in His timing.
- **Seasonal Reflection:** Reflect on the different seasons of your life and how God has been faithful through each one. Trust that He will continue to guide you.

Prayer:
"Lord, help me to trust Your timing and to surrender my plans to You. May I find peace knowing that You are in control and Your timing is perfect? In Jesus' name, Amen."

Sabbath Practice:

- **Seasonal Journal:** Keep a journal of the different seasons in your life. Reflect on God's faithfulness and timing in each season.

Reflect and Renew:
Trusting God's timing brings peace and assurance. Surrender your plans to Him and rest in the knowledge that He is in control.

5th Sunday Reflection 6: The Comfort of God's Presence

Scripture Verse:
Psalm 23:4 (ESV) - "Even though I walk through the valley of the shadow of death, I will fear no evil, for you are with me; your rod and your staff, they comfort me."

Reflection:

Psalm 23:4 assures us of God's presence and comfort, even in the darkest times. Knowing that God is with us brings peace and removes fear. The Sabbath is an opportunity to rest in God's presence and to find comfort in His unfailing love.

Practical Application:

- **Comfort Prayer:** Spend time in prayer, seeking God's comfort and presence in any areas of fear or anxiety.
- **Support Others:** Reach out to someone who may need comfort. Offer a listening ear, a kind word, or a prayer.

Prayer:

"Lord, thank You for Your comforting presence. Help me to rest in Your love and to find peace in knowing that You are always with me. In Jesus' name, Amen."

Sabbath Practice:

- **Comfort Reflection:** Think about times when God has comforted you and thank Him for His presence and faithfulness.

Reflect and Renew:

God's presence brings comfort and peace. Rest in His unfailing love and trust that He is always with you, even in the darkest times.

5th Sunday Reflection 7: The Strength of Community

Scripture Verse:

Hebrews 10:24-25 (ESV) - "And let us consider how to stir up one another to love and good works, not neglecting to meet together, as is the habit of some, but encouraging one another, and all the more as you see the Day drawing near."

Reflection:

Hebrews 10:24-25 emphasizes the importance of community and mutual encouragement. Being part of a supportive community strengthens our faith and motivates us to love and do good work. The Sabbath is a time to connect with our community and to build one another up.

Practical Application:

- **Community Engagement:** Get involved in your church or faith community. Participate in group activities, worship, and service projects.
- **Encouragement Notes:** Write notes of encouragement to members of your community. Let them know you appreciate and support them.

Prayer:

"Lord, thank You for the gift of community. Help me to be an active and supportive member of my faith community, encouraging others and building them up in love. In Jesus' name, Amen."

Sabbath Practice:

- **Community Gathering:** Host or attend a community gathering. Use this time to connect, share, and support one another.

Reflect and Renew:

A supportive community strengthens our faith and encourages us to love and work well. Embrace the strength of community and find joy in building one another up.

5th Sunday Reflection 8: The Peace of Surrender

Scripture Verse:

Philippians 4:6-7 (ESV) - "Do not be anxious about anything, but in everything by prayer and supplication with thanksgiving let your requests be made known to God. And the peace of God, which surpasses all understanding, will guard your hearts and minds in Christ Jesus."

Reflection:

Philippians 4:6-7 encourages us to surrender our anxieties to God through prayer and thanksgiving. Surrendering our worries brings us the peace of God, which guards our hearts and minds. The Sabbath is an opportunity to practice surrender and to find peace in God's presence.

Practical Application:

- **Prayer of Surrender:** Spend time in prayer, surrendering your worries and anxieties to God. Trust Him to bring you peace.
- **Gratitude List:** Create a list of things you are thankful for. Use this list to shift your focus from worries to blessings.

Prayer:

"Lord, help me to surrender my anxieties to You and to trust in Your peace. May Your peace guard my heart and mind, bringing me rest and comfort. In Jesus' name, Amen."

Sabbath Practice:

- **Peaceful Reflection:** Dedicate part of your Sabbath to peaceful reflection. Meditate on Philippians 4:6-7 and let God's peace fill your heart.

Reflect and Renew:

Surrendering our worries to God brings peace and rest. Trust in His presence and let His peace guard your heart and mind.

5th Sunday Reflection 9: The Joy of Worship

Scripture Verse:

Psalm 95:1-2 (ESV) - "Oh come, let us sing to the LORD; let us make a joyful noise to the rock of our salvation! Let us come into his presence with thanksgiving; let us make a joyful noise to him with songs of praise!"

Reflection:

Psalm 95:1-2 invites us to come into God's presence with joyful worship. Singing praises and giving thanks brings joy to our hearts and honors God. The Sabbath is a perfect time to engage in joyful worship and to celebrate God's goodness.

Practical Application:

- **Joyful Singing:** Include joyful singing in your worship. Choose songs that celebrate God's goodness and bring joy to your heart.
- **Worship Art:** Express your worship through art. Create something that reflects your praise and thanksgiving to God.

Prayer:

"Lord, thank You for the joy of worship. Help me to come into Your presence with joyful songs and a thankful heart. May my worship honor You and bring joy to my soul. In Jesus' name, Amen."

Sabbath Practice:

- **Joyful Worship:** Dedicate part of your Sabbath to joyful worship. Sing, dance, or create art to express your praise to God.

Reflect and Renew:

Joyful worship brings us closer to God and fills our hearts with His joy. Celebrate His goodness, and let your worship be a joyful expression of praise.

5th Sunday Reflection 10: The Strength of Hope

Scripture Verse:

Romans 15:13 (ESV) - "May the God of hope fill you with all joy and peace in believing, so that by the power of the Holy Spirit you may abound in hope."

Reflection:

Romans 15:13 speaks of the strength and joy that comes from hope. Hope in God fills us with joy and peace, empowering us through the Holy Spirit. The Sabbath is a time to renew our hope in God and to find strength in His promises.

Practical Application:

- **Hope Journal:** Keep a journal of your hopes and God's promises. Reflect on how His promises give you strength and joy.
- **Hopeful Actions:** Engage in activities that bring hope to others. Encourage someone who is struggling or participates in a community service project.

Prayer:

"Lord, thank You for the hope You give. Fill me with joy and peace as I trust in Your promises. May Your hope strengthen and empower me through the Holy Spirit. In Jesus' name, Amen."

Sabbath Practice:

- **Hope Reflection:** Spend time reflecting on your hope in God. Meditate on Romans 15:13 and let His hope fill your heart.

Reflect and Renew:

Hope in God brings strength and joy. Renew your hope in His promises and let His hope empower you through the Holy Spirit.

5th Sunday Reflection 11: The Peace of God's Word

Scripture Verse:

Psalm 119:165 (ESV) - "Great peace have those who love your law; nothing can make them stumble."

Reflection:

Psalm 119:165 emphasizes the peace that comes from loving God's Word. Engaging with Scripture brings clarity, guidance, and peace to our lives. The Sabbath is an ideal time to immerse ourselves in God's Word and to find rest in His teachings.

Practical Application:

- **Scripture Study:** Dedicate time to studying God's Word. Choose a passage to read, meditate on, and apply to your life.

- **Bible Journaling:** Keep a journal of your reflections on Scripture. Write down insights, prayers, and applications from your study.

Prayer:
"Lord, thank You for the peace that comes from Your Word. Help me to love Your law and to find rest in Your teachings. May Your Word guide and comfort me. In Jesus' name, Amen."

Sabbath Practice:

- **Scripture Immersion:** Spend part of your Sabbath immersed in Scripture. Read, meditate, and journal on passages that bring you peace.

Reflect and Renew:
Loving God's Word brings great peace. Immerse yourself in Scripture and let His teachings guide and comfort you.

5th Sunday Reflection 12: The Joy of Serving

Scripture Verse:
1 Peter 4:10 (ESV) - "As each has received a gift, use it to serve one another, as good stewards of God's varied grace."

Reflection:
1 Peter 4:10 encourages us to use our gifts to serve others. Serving with our God-given talents brings joy and fulfills our calling as stewards of His grace. The Sabbath is a wonderful time to reflect on how we can serve others and to find joy in using our gifts for God's glory.

Practical Application:

- **Gift Inventory:** Take an inventory of your gifts and talents. Reflect on how you can use them to serve others and glorify God.
- **Service Project:** Participate in a service project. Use your skills to help those in need and to contribute to your community.

Prayer:
"Lord, thank You for the gifts You have given me. Help me to use them to serve others and to bring glory to Your name. May I find joy in being a good steward of Your grace? In Jesus' name, Amen."

Sabbath Practice:

- **Service Reflection:** Dedicate part of your Sabbath to reflecting on your gifts and how you can serve others. Make a plan to use your talents in service.

Reflect and Renew:
Serving with our gifts brings joy and fulfills our calling as stewards of God's grace. Reflect on how you can use your talents to serve others and find joy in being a blessing to those around you.

Concluding thoughts:

Dear Reader,

Thank you for joining me on this journey through "Sabbath Rest Finding Peace and Reflection in God's Presence." Over the past year, I hope and pray that you have found true rest and meaningful reflection each week. As we have explored the depths of Sabbath rest together, I trust that you have experienced a renewed connection with God, a deeper sense of peace, and a greater appreciation for the rhythms of rest He has designed for us.

This devotional was created to help you embrace the gift of Sabbath rest. From understanding its biblical foundations to implementing practical steps in your daily life, each week was intended to draw you closer to God and enrich your spiritual journey. I hope you have found the reflections, prayers, and practices helpful and transformative. I pray these experiences have brought you peace, clarity, and profound spiritual growth and renewal.

Consider the changes you have witnessed as you reflect on the past year. Have you found yourself more in tune with God's presence? Have the weekly reflections helped you to navigate life's challenges with a deeper sense of trust and surrender? These are the fruits of a consistent and heartfelt practice of Sabbath rest, and I hope they have become evident in your life.

I welcome your comments and feedback on how to make this journey even more meaningful. Your insights and experiences are invaluable. Sharing what worked for you, what challenges you faced, and how you overcame them can help refine this devotional for others. I believe our collective experiences can create a richer, more impactful resource for those seeking to deepen their relationship with God.

I would love to hear about your journey over the past year. What moments stood out to you? How have the themes and reflections resonated with your walk of faith? Hearing your stories brings joy to my heart and fosters a sense of community. It reminds us that we are all on this journey together, learning and growing in our faith and understanding of God's rest.

Please feel free to reach out and share your thoughts and stories. Please email me at the7thday@gmail.com. Your journey is important to me, and I look forward to hearing from you. Let us continue to support one another in our pursuit of rest and reflection, continually finding peace in God's presence. Together, we can build a community that values and practices the rhythms of rest God has graciously provided us.

Sincerely,

Michael Stowe

THIS SECTION LISTS all the scripture references used in "Sabbath Rest Finding Peace and Reflection in God's Presence," drawn from the Bible's English Standard Version (ESV). "ESV.Org." n.d. ESV Bible. https://www.esv.org/.

January: The Foundation of Rest

1. Genesis 2:2-3
2. Exodus 20:8-11
3. Mark 2:27
4. Luke 13:10-17
5. John 5:1-18

February: Trusting in God's Timing

1. Ecclesiastes 3:1

2. Psalm 37:7
3. Isaiah 40:31
4. Lamentations 3:25-26
5. Romans 8:28

March: Jesus and the Sabbath

1. Matthew 11:28-30
2. Mark 2:27-28
3. Luke 4:16
4. John 7:23
5. Hebrews 4:9-11

5th Sunday Reflections

1. Psalm 46:10
2. Ephesians 4:32
3. Psalm 19:1
4. 2 Corinthians 9:7
5. Ecclesiastes 3:1
6. Psalm 23:4
7. Hebrews 10:24-25
8. Philippians 4:6-7
9. Psalm 95:1-2
10. Romans 15:13
11. Psalm 119:165
12. 1 Peter 4:10

ADDITIONAL WEEKLY REFLECTIONS

1. Zephaniah 3:17
2. Psalm 92:1-4
3. 1 Thessalonians 5:16-18
4. James 1:17
5. Acts 2:42-47
6. Hebrews 10:24-25
7. Galatians 6:2
8. 1 Thessalonians 5:11
9. Hebrews 4:9-10
10. Revelation 14:13
11. Matthew 25:34
12. Revelation 21:3-4

Using This Reference

Use this reference to revisit the scripture verses included in each reflection. Studying these passages within their broader biblical context can deepen your understanding and enhance your spiritual journey.

Also by Michael Stowe

Journey to Bethlehem: 24 Days of Advent Reflection
Lenten Reflections
Sabbath Rest Finding Peace and Reflection in God's Presence

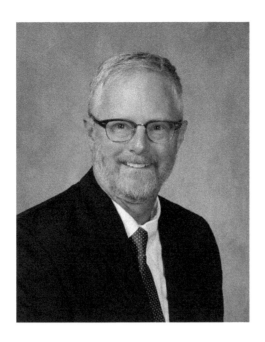

About the Author

Dr. Michael Stowe, a distinguished academic and professor, has dedicated his life to exploring theological depths and the nuanced study of Christian thought. A respected member of Cross Lutheran Church, his journey in faith and personal research in scripture and theology reflects a strong commitment to understanding Christian belief.

Milton Keynes UK
Ingram Content Group UK Ltd.
UKHW032125201024
449815UK00011B/100